MIRROR IMAGE

Unless otherwise noted, all Scripture quotations are from the Holy Bible, New International Version of the Bible. Copyright © 1973, 1978, 1984, 2011 by Biblica, Inc. Used by permission.

Scripture quotations marked NKJV are from the New King James Version of the Bible. Copyright © 1979, 1980, 1982 by Thomas Nelson, Inc., publishers. Used by permission.

Scripture quotations marked (CEV) are from the Contemporary English Version Copyright © 1991, 1992, 1995 by American Bible Society, Used by Permission.

Scripture quotations marked NLT are from the Holy Bible, New Living Translation. Copyright © 2007. Used by permission of Tyndale House Publishers, Inc., Wheaton, IL 60189. All rights reserved.

Scripture quotations marked MSG are from The Message: The Bible in Contemporary English. Copyright © 1993, 1994, 1995, 1996, 2000, 2001, 2002. Used by permission of NavPress Publishing Group.

Scripture quotations marked ESV are from the Holy Bible, English Standard Version. Copyright © 2001 by Crossway Bibles, a division of Good News Publishers. Used by permission.

Scripture quotations marked TPT are from The Passion Translation®. Copyright © 2017, 2018 by Passion & Fire Ministries, Inc. Used by permission. All rights reserved. ThePassionTranslation.com.

Scripture quotations taken from the Amplified® Bible (AMPC), Copyright © 1954, 1958, 1962, 1964, 1965, 1987 by The Lockman Foundation. Used by permission. www.Lockman.org
Scripture quotations marked KJV are from the Holy Bible, King James Version, public domain.

Copyright © 2017 by Mercy UK. Second edition 2019. All rights reserved.

Principal author (UK Edition): Arianna Walker

Line Art Illustrations: Aimee Wood. Visit the artist's instagram: @bloommydear_

Every effort has been made to provide accurate information at the time of publication, neither the publisher nor the author assumes any responsibility for errors or for changes that occur after publication.

Printed without cost to Mercy UK through a strategic partnership with ClearView Baptist Church, Franklin, Nashville, TN. A message from our sponsor:

"Our motive in partnering with Mercy UK is to further the power and truths set forth by Jesus Christ and to set captives free. Therefore, we believe in partnerships which further that cause. Kingdom work is always better when done together."

Endorsements

"This book is packed with fresh insight on self-image. In reading it, I was reminded of the unhelpful lies we so readily buy into on a daily basis, and steered towards life-giving Truth. A brilliantly practical and uplifting resource."

- Philippa Hanna

"Mirror Image has been written for all those who find themselves imprisoned by fears, doubts and insecurities. Arianna writes each chapter with a heart that wants to embrace, encourage, inspire and celebrate the real you that God sees. This book will give you a true reflection of your real beauty and value. Be free!"

- Charlotte Gambill

"The impact of image and identity are key things we need to understand. In my work as a Consultant Psychiatrist, I see how mental ill-health and distress can be caused by a lack of identity and by chasing after unhelpful images of the 'ideal' self. In this updated book, Arianna Walker tackles these issues head-on. Arianna unpacks many of the do's and don'ts that psychology offers us, but also signposts the reader in unpacking issues of faith and in receiving our sense of identity from the ultimate Image-Giver."

- Dr Rob Waller

"Mirror Image is an amazing book for every woman. It's easy to read, and full of hope and powerful God truths about our worth, value and self image. A MUST READ!! For all us girls!"

- Anna Smith

Dedication

This book is dedicated to every woman who thinks that she is less than she is; every woman who feels lost, broken or beyond the reach of the Father's love. May the pages of this book help you to know that God sees you; that He has plans to prosper you and not to harm you, and plans to give you hope and a future.

With thanks

Thank you to every Mercy UK graduate whose stories and artwork fill the pages of this book with the power of transformed lives - you are my heroes.

Thank you to Nancy Alcorn whose incredible leadership, vision and faith-filled determination has been and will continue to be an incredible source of inspiration to me. You are a true hero of the faith and it is an honour to serve you.

Thank you to my amazing team - the people who day after day labour alongside me to build Mercy UK and increase its reach so that more people can live a life of freedom and hope through a relationship with Jesus. You are all reflections of Him - you have become the mirror.

Thanks to those who helped me to make this book a reality - proofreading, editing, constructive criticism and eye to detail have made all the difference.

Thank you to ClearView Baptist Church, Franklin, TN, for your generous sponsorship of this resource. Without your partnership, the printing of this book and the accompanying 'Reflections Cards' would not have been possible.

And finally to my Father - words are not enough and so instead I will live from a grateful heart all the days of my life to bring glory to your Name.

All proceeds from the sale of this book go towards the work of Mercy UK.

Contents

Preface   **10**
Tell Her She is Looking in the Wrong Mirror

Introduction   **12**
Forgetting What We Look Like

Chapter 1   **16**
Dare to Bare:
The Dressing Room Mirror

Chapter 2   **32**
Don't Look Back:
The Rear-View Mirror

Chapter 3   **46**
Because You're Worth it:
The Full Length Mirror

Chapter 4   **64**
Who's the Fairest of Them All:
The Dance Studio Mirror

Chapter 5   **78**
Tales of the Unexpected:
The Shop Window Mirror

Chapter 6   **96**
Know, Believe, Do:
The Compact Mirror

Chapter 7   **110**
Becoming the Mirror

Mirror Image
Tell Her She is Looking in the Wrong Mirror

─────

She was 17 years old. Tears streamed down her face as she lifted her eyes to meet mine. "I have an eating disorder," she whispered, barely audible.

I touched her arm and asked her how long she had been suffering for. She shrugged, "Years, on and off. I look in the mirror and I hate what I see." Taken aback, I asked her what she saw when she looked in the mirror. Her reply has haunted me ever since, "I look in the mirror and see a fat, ugly girl who is worthless and deserves to die."

It was then that I heard the whisper of the Holy Spirit, "Tell her she is looking in the wrong mirror. Tell her that she is believing a false reflection and that I will show her a true reflection, if she chooses to look."

That conversation happened over a decade ago and since then, through the work of Mercy UK, I have seen God reveal to person after person, the power that comes from believing Truth over lies; the freedom that comes with putting that Truth into action and the beauty of a true reflection in the mirror of God's Word.

Mercy UK is committed to the fulfilment of Isaiah 61 to:

─── *Isaiah 61*

"bind up the broken-hearted, set the captives free, release prisoners from darkness... and comfort those who mourn in Zion"

Isaiah 61 ───────────────────────────────────

and not just through our free-of-charge residential home or young women aged 18 to around 30. Mercy UK works in partnership with local churches across the UK to see hope restored and lives transformed through our people-helper training, resources and our 8-week Keys to Freedom discipleship course empowering every Christian to live free and stay free.

To this day, that young woman I met years before we opened the doors of Mercy UK is still in my thoughts and prayers. I wonder where she is, what she is doing and if she ever pulled through.

I don't even know her name, yet she had a lasting impact on me and set me on a journey that now has me sitting at a desk writing a book that began with that conversation. If you're out there, I hope you get to read this one day.

- Arianna Walker, 2019

Forgetting What We Look Like

Remember the old hall of mirrors you used to get at fairgrounds? Those mirrors that distort your image? Each mirror shows you a distortion of your true reflection and the absurdity of the image is hilarious - we walk away and laugh at the reflections because we know they are false.

But life can be like those halls of mirrors - we are constantly bombarded with images (there are over ten million photographs uploaded to Facebook alone every hour) and reflections of ourselves, these mirrors try to show us who we are and what we look like, but the truth is that many of those images are tainted, distorted like the hall of mirrors at a fairground. Sadly, unlike the fairground, many of us don't walk away laughing, because we believe the false image to be true. Over time, these false reflections begin to affect everything we do; how we relate to others, the decisions we make, our thinking patterns, coping mechanisms and even the future we are believing for.

It wasn't long after my conversation with that heartbroken young woman I described earlier that I turned to James 1:22-25 (NIV) and read the following passage:

James 1:22-25 (NIV)

"Do not merely listen to the word, and so deceive yourselves. Do what it says. Anyone who listens to the word but does not do what it says is like someone who looks at his face in a mirror and, after looking at himself, goes away and immediately forgets what he looks like. But whoever looks intently into the perfect law that gives freedom, and continues in it—not forgetting what they have heard, but doing it—they will be blessed in what they do."

James 1:22-25 (NIV)

It got me thinking about the amount of times I have looked in the mirror and disliked what I saw, the times when I have forgotten who I am and about the One who made me. James tells us that God's mirror leads to blessings and freedom. Therefore, it's safe to assume that these false mirrors will do the opposite; they will trap us, hold us captive and steal our blessing. They will make us forget what we look like.

I want to invite you to come on a journey with me; a journey that will uncover some of the false mirrors you may be looking in, and show you your true reflection in God's mirror. Once we expose these 'false reflections' in our lives, it gives us the knowledge and therefore the power to make informed choices about which mirrors we look in and how to recognise the trap of:

- The dressing room mirror and the masks we wear
- The rear-view mirror and the pull to our past
- The full-length mirror and the lie of self-esteem
- The dance studio mirror of comparison
- The filtered selfie-lens of perfection
- The shop window reflection and the unwelcome sting of the unexpected

On this journey, we want to delve into the real questions and the raw issues that we face in today's society. Never before has it been so easy to filter our faces or fill our bodies with silicone, botox, fast-foods and diet pills, all in an attempt to keep up appearances. But we are chasing an illusion; like a promised pot of gold at the end of each rainbow, these false mirrors have us pursuing every shimmering and shining image of perfection. But, as the saying goes, all that glitters is not gold. It is time to challenge these false reflections and begin the daring adventure of removing our masks and taking the risk to reveal our authentic selves.

But more than that, it's time to take a long hard look at our true reflection in the compact mirror that is the Word of God and resist the temptation to avoid even our own eye contact in the mirror, to not turn away or compare, condemn or criticise the image before us. As we bravely embrace who we are, we will find that the treasure we've all been looking for has been with us all along. This treasure holds the power to make our lives rich because quite simply, it's hidden within that most precious place of intimacy with the Lord;

Isaiah 33:6 (TPT)

"He will be your constant source of stability in changing times, and out of his abundant love he gives you the riches of salvation, wisdom, and knowledge. Yes, the fear of the Lord is the key to this treasure!"

Isaiah 33:6 (TPT)

So let me ask you, what mirror are you looking in today?
Who is staring back at you? The real you, or a false reflection?
What lengths will you go to to fit in or look the part?

Many of these mirrors are ones that I have identified from my own journey and from working with women for many years now. I believe there are simple tools available to us that will enable us to break free from false reflections and into a revelation of the true reflection God's mirror presents to us. This book will unpack these tools and will offer you easy to follow advice and practical wisdom as well as inspiring stories of women who have discovered these truths for themselves and are living from a place of freedom.

Along with this book, our devotional style Mirror Image 'Reflections Cards' are designed to help you find your feet and take strong steps forward in forging your own path to authenticity through creative expression, scriptural study and personal reflection within the context of your relationship with God.

There are a number of ways you can use these resources. The book can be read as a single resource or, if you want to go deeper, you can read this book alongside the reflections cards to help you unpack all that you are learning, enabling revelation to become transformation.

My hope is that this book, and the resources that go with it, become a catalyst for permanent change in your life and that it sets you off on a journey of discovering the wonderful freedom that comes from knowing who you are.

Let me pray for you:
Holy Spirit, I ask that each reader who invests the time to read and interact with the contents of this book will be met by Your Presence. I pray that she will feel Your gentle guidance as You bring her to revelation and Truth about herself, her identity and her worth. I pray that Truth will enter her heart and mind and as it does so, that the Truth would set her free.

In Jesus' Name, Amen.

Chapter 1
Dare to Bare:
The Dressing Room Mirror

──────

Imagine the classic image of a dressing room mirror, surrounded by light bulbs. A performing artist is seated in front of it, covering her face with a thick mask of make-up to help her adopt a persona and deliver the star performance everyone expects. As the make-up goes on, so does the mask - she begins the process of covering herself up, hiding who she really is, so the people watching can see who she wants them to see.

──────────────── /mɑːsk/ ────────────────
'A covering for all or part of the face,
worn to conceal one's true identity'.

Many of us do that exact thing every day. We put on a false mask and become who we need to be to give the performance expected of us. This is the 'dressing room mirror.' It represents the mirror of our fake identity, our carefully constructed cover-up.

Hiding behind a false identity by wearing masks, is a natural reaction to pain and is often used as a defence mechanism to express our hurt or to protect ourselves from more hurt. These behaviours become masks that cover our real identities.

If you look into a mirror while wearing a mask, the reflection does not show your true face. It is the same with the mirror of God's Word; if we wear a mask, we hide ourselves from its Truth. In order to see the Truth that can set us free, we must remove every mask that prevents us from discovering our true reflection.

Hiding ourselves is a natural human reaction to guilt, shame and pain. In Genesis 3:7-11 (NLT) we see Adam and Eve's immediate reaction to their choice to disobey God. It says:

Genesis 3:7-11 (NLT)

"At that moment their eyes were opened, and they suddenly felt shame at their nakedness. So they sewed fig leaves together to cover themselves. When the cool evening breezes were blowing, the man and his wife heard the Lord God walking about in the garden. So they hid from the Lord God among the trees. Then the Lord God called to the man, "Where are you?" He replied, "I heard you walking in the garden, so I hid. I was afraid because I was naked."

Genesis 3:7-11 (NLT)

Adam and Eve hid from God because of their guilt and shame. God asked them where they were, not because He didn't know, but because He can only begin to work with us when we are prepared to step out and reveal exactly where we are.

When you are lost and call someone for directions, the very first question they will ask is 'where are you?'. In order for us to receive direction and input from God, He needs to know that we are prepared to accurately describe our present location, no matter how far from the right track it may appear to be.

When Adam and Eve hid, covering themselves with leaves, they effectively found themselves before a 'dressing room mirror.' It's as if they painted on fake smiles, covering over the blemishes and ugly pimples on their lives that they were suddenly so aware and ashamed of.

It's interesting to note that Adam and Eve covered their most intimate parts with leaves. We all do the same when we hide from God; we hide our most intimate parts and fear Him seeing us naked.

But God created us to be revealed before Him, because in Him we have nothing to be ashamed of. There is often a cycle of shame, fear and control at work that causes us to want to hide. We can see that in the scripture when Adam said: 'I was afraid because I was naked, so I hid myself. 'We might recognise it as: 'I am afraid that you will find out about the real me, how dysfunctional I really am, how ashamed I am, so I will control how close you get to me, or I will control what part of me you see.'

If we want freedom and wholeness, we must be prepared to lay ourselves bare before God.

Shame, fear, and control are primary forces that work against us and will try to stop us from trusting God and so damage our intimacy and walk with Him.

Psalm 139 (MSG)

"God, investigate my life; get all the facts first-hand. I'm an open book to You; even from a distance, You know what I'm thinking. You know when I leave and when I get back; I'm never out of Your sight. You know everything I'm going to say before I start the first sentence. I look behind me and You're there, then up ahead and You're there, too - your reassuring presence, coming and going. This is too much, too wonderful - I can't take it all in!

Psalm 139 (MSG)

Investigate my life, O God, find out everything about me; Cross examine and test me, get a clear picture of what I'm about; See for Yourself whether I've done anything wrong - then guide me on the road to eternal life."

King David understood this when he wrote Psalm 139 (MSG): David dared to bare himself before God, not because he thought he was perfect but because he understood that in order for God to do His work he had to invite God in and give Him an 'access-all-areas' pass.

When God asked Adam and Eve to reveal themselves, He saw that they had tried to make their own coverings. They had sewn together fig leaves to cover their shame and no doubt they had made a poor attempt at self-protection. God in His kindness and in His mercy responded to their courage to come out of hiding by spilling the blood of an animal and making coverings for them (Genesis 3:21).

The first blood spilled on the earth was to cover Adam and Eve's shame. It's so powerful to remember that Jesus's blood was spilled for the same reason. To cover our sin and shame once and for all, to invite us out into the open, and to let the love and forgiveness of God cover us, so we don't need to cover ourselves.

_____ *2 Corinthians 3:18 (CEV)*

"So our faces are not covered. They show the bright glory of the Lord, as the Lord's Spirit makes us more and more like our glorious Lord."

2 Corinthians 3:18 (CEV) _____

So, the question is this - will you dare to bare? Are you ready to take a look in the dressing room mirror? Let's start with identifying some of the common masks we use to hide ourselves behind.

The Mask of Perfectionism and Performance

⎯⎯

This mask sounds like: 'I must not show any weakness, failure, or struggle of any kind because I am a Christian, a leader, an example and I have to maintain the picture perfect image that people have of me. ' Or it may sound like: 'I have to earn love and respect, so I will perform and become all that is expected of me, never showing anyone my weaknesses.

Yet I know that I am weak and therefore doomed to failure, so I must try harder, be better and keep improving myself. '

In other words, doing good equals being good. This is a false identity, a mask that will stop God being able to get close. Not only that, but people will struggle to get close too. It's actually prideful to think that we can be even anywhere near perfect this side of heaven, or to think that we can impress God with our goodness, our works, our ability to perfect ourselves, or our success.

The fact is none of us are perfect, no matter how hard we try. God is not a strict teacher who points out our faults, so then we can go and fix everything and then present ourselves to Him for the next fault to be worked on. God sees past our imperfections and our failings and in His love chooses to use our lives for great things anyway. When you look at many of the characters in the Bible who achieved great things, they were definitely far from perfect.

The Apostle Paul was someone who understood weakness. In 2 Corinthians he mentions a 'tormentor', a thorn in his flesh that he asked God to remove three times. He records God's answer in

2 Corinthians 12:9 (NIV)

"Each time he said, "My grace is all you need. My power works best in weakness. " So now I am glad to boast about my weaknesses, so that the power of Christ can work through me."

2 Corinthians 12:9 (NIV)

Paul understood that **weakness isn't something to fear; we are simply not designed to live in our own strength.** We don't need to strive for perfection because our weakness gives God the opportunity to demonstrate the fullness of his strength in our lives. Yes, work together with the Holy Spirit to grow and learn as a person but do not expect ever to reach perfection and don't beat yourself up when you fail.

The Victim Mask

The mask of the 'victim' is another that we can allow to cover our lives. It sounds like this; 'Nothing ever works out for me; I always get disappointed; people will always let me down; I might as well not even try because I'll just get hurt.' Victim mentality tells us that we have a right to be a victim, that it's everyone else's fault and therefore we carry no responsibility towards our freedom.

Some don't want to remove the victim mask because without it there's no excuse for not trying, for not taking responsibility for their own choices, and for the path they choose to walk. This mask protects against the fear of failure because a 'victim' thinks failure is all that can be expected from them. **The victim mask tells us that there is no hope, there is no chance of living free and not even God can fix us, so what is the point of even trying?**

A 'victim' believes their problems are a result of what has happened to them and no-one can change that. Not even God! Some of us have lived with our conditions, issues and behaviours for so long that we develop an attachment to them. A 'victim' fears removing the mask. They don't know who they are without their issue or problem to define them.

A victim mentality asks, "Will people still be my friend if I don't need them to pray for me, give support and rally round me all the time?" To be free from this mask we must be prepared to let go of the past, which is described in more detail later in this book.

The Mask of Inadequacy

Moses told God he couldn't speak; Gideon was convinced he was a weak man, not the warrior that God had called him to be; Saul hid in the baggage when he was meant to be anointed as King. All of these men who did incredible exploits for God, at first, hid behind the mask of inadequacy as a reason for God not to call upon them. The leaders God chose to spearhead some of His greatest moves struggled with inadequacy.

Inadequacy is a mask many people wear that keeps God from being able to use us. The fact is that we are small, we are inadequate and we will always be inadequate and unworthy for what God calls us to do. It is not our adequacy or worthiness that causes Him to use us, it's His adequacy and His worthiness. **We have to stop looking to ourselves, our own strength, our own abilities and instead look to His strength and grace that will work through us.**

When He uses us for His purposes, it's never because of who we are and what we can do but who He is and what He can do through us. When we complain to God about our inadequacy, it only shows that we are looking to our own strength and not His strength in us. Taking off the mask of inadequacy means we look to God for what we do not have and recognise that God delights to show His power through the imperfect. In fact, it is our imperfections that create space for God's power to be manifested.

Did you know that what distinguishes a genuine pearl from a fake one is its imperfections? It's the irregular sphere, the faint sense of grit on the surface of the genuine pearl that sets it apart from the counterfeit smoothness of a fake one; and it is by this imperfection that it's value is found. In the same way, it's our imperfections that give us authenticity as a human being.

The Mask of Independence

'I must make it on my own; people have left me, hurt me, abandoned me, God has disappointed me, so I will do this thing called life alone, without anyone's help. You can't count on anyone but yourself'. So speaks the mask of independence.

This mask will allow you to control how close people get to you by making you believe that no one can ultimately be trusted and therefore you must protect yourself. People do this by building up an internal barrier; although it succeeds in keeping people out, it has the unfortunate side effect of keeping you locked behind it, isolated and alone. Independence does not like to show vulnerability or need and so this mask will cause you to suffer alone, silent, behind a self-made wall of growing anger and frustration, yet not being prepared to reach out for help.

The Mask of Sarcasm, Bitterness, Criticism and Blame

This mask will use any of the above to put others down (in the case of sarcasm, we can put others down and get a laugh!), but the underlying motivation is to make us feel better about ourselves. We find fault with others to reconcile the faults in ourselves that we are desperately trying to hide. This mask acts like a reflective shield by deflecting unwanted attention but it also cleverly and tactically defends your self esteem and value by tearing others down.

The Mask of a Lively Personality

Clearly, some people genuinely have a lively, life and soul of the party personality type; it is not a mask to them. On the other hand, there are those who wear this personality like a mask, aware that their smile hides the pain inside.

I once watched an interview with the singer Robbie Williams. He had just performed an incredible show to over 80,000 people. Alone on the stage, he held their attention by performing some of his best hits in addition to laughing, joking and being all they wanted him to be. "Let me entertain you" he sang and the crowd cheered him on.

But after the show was over, he sat in front of the camera and revealed a rare look behind the mask. Asked by the interviewer whether he enjoyed the show, he shrugged and said that it was just a show.

His eyes revealed a sad discontent, he said it was a personality he put on to be able to do what he does, but underneath it all he would swap it in a heartbeat to find happiness, peace and contentment. He admitted he wore a mask, a fake smile to hide the pain.

The Mask of Passivity

This mask will make you feel safe by doing nothing. It's the same defence mechanism many animals use; the ostrich buries her head in the sand in the hope that the threat will leave; the opossum plays dead for the same reason and the potato beetle larva simply covers itself in its own toxic excrement to create a stench so bad nothing will come close!

Doing nothing means you at least can't be blamed for failing. If you never try to build close relationships, you can't be rejected; if you don't take the test, you can't fail it; if you don't expect anything, you won't be disappointed.

If you never even try, then you will not have to face the pain of knowing that your effort wasn't good enough. This mask will lead you to live your life as a passive bystander, watching the world go by while you find a level of comfort in the smallness of your world because there is at least no risk attached.

The Mask of "I'm too Busy"

────

This mask is too busy to face up to itself; too busy doing things for God, for other people. The bonus of this mask is that we don't even have to feel guilty about not facing ourselves, God, or anyone else because busyness means at least we are getting things done! We hide from what matters by filling our time with what doesn't, yet we convince ourselves that all this busyness is legitimate, necessary and therefore justified.

If the motivation behind your busyness is to keep the attention off yourself and to distract yourself from facing the issues you need to address, then it is a mask.

Revelation is not Transformation

────

You may have read through the list of masks and had a revelation that one (or more) of them applies to you. That's great, but don't let it end there. Having a revelation about something means that a truth has been revealed to you, which is great but it is only step one!

You can have a revelation but it won't be transformation until something is done about it, follow your breakthrough with walk-through. Take another step on the journey: peel off the mask; come out of hiding; dare to bare.

Queen Esther wore a mask for many years. Her true identity as a poor, orphaned Jewish girl was hidden from those around her and, for a season, this false identity protected her and kept her safe. There may be times in our lives when God will allow us to wear our masks for a reason and for a season; a time where we choose to hide ourselves to stay safe like Esther did.

Yet, there came a time in Esther's life when she was presented with a choice. A time when the consequences of keeping the mask would affect not just her but an entire nation. This was no longer just about her life: the King, her husband, was going to give a command for her own people, the Jews to be killed. The lives of thousands of people depended on her being brave enough to take off the mask and reveal her true identity to those around her. Would she have the courage to do it? Could she dare to bare?

Esther's first reaction was fear - she could be killed if she approached the King uninvited, especially to tell him that she was, in fact, one of the people he had sentenced to death. But her uncle Mordecai says this in reply to her fears:

_____ Esther 4:12-14 (NIV)

'When Esther's words were reported to Mordecai, he sent back this answer: "Do not think that because you are in the king's house you alone of all the Jews will escape. For if you remain silent at this time, relief and deliverance for the Jews will arise from another place, but you and your father's family will perish. And who knows but that you have come to royal position for such a time as this?"'

Esther 4:12-14 (NIV) _____

God is calling time on the masks that you are hiding behind. Will you have the courage to peel them off, to be real and transparent? You see, there are people who need you to be who you are called to be. They need you to step into your true identity in Christ, so that you can lead them to safety. There are many people who will be reached by your courage to strip the masks off your life, just as in Esther's life.

Like Esther, you have a choice, but remember Mordecai's words because they are written for us all to listen to. God will surely reach those who you are meant to reach in some other way. He will accomplish all that he has purposed in his people's lives with or without you. But the effects of not removing the masks will affect firstly your own life and then those whose lives you have a direct impact on: maybe your partner, children, family or friends.

Taking off a mask, a false identity, can feel a little like having surgery. When I gave birth to my children, I had to have surgery to get them out. I've had two caesarean sections, so I know from personal experience how painful and frightening surgery can be. But in the end, being cut and my flesh being exposed (with no clothes allowed to cover up and hide behind during surgery!) brought forth new life. Going through that painful process brought a new beginning to my life; it released a whole new expression of a part of me that had not been seen before: motherhood.

In the same way that we experience surgery physically, we can experience surgery at an emotional and spiritual level. God is a master surgeon and He specialises in internal heart surgery. He is the expert, and yes, it can be painful and frightening but it is part of the process. I believe that allowing Him access to all the areas of our hearts and choosing to remove the mask so He can get close enough, will mean new life; a new season and a whole new expression of a part of you that is waiting for its moment to shine.

Let's get practical

So let me ask, are you wearing masks? If so, what are they and are you prepared to remove them? Are you ready to look into the mirror of God's Word without the layers of self-protection?

And if so, then let's do something about it! This part of each chapter is to help you implement actual change in your everyday life to see a reflection that is true and from the Father.

Letting go of the Masks

Part of removing the masks you wear is about being honest with God and others around you about how you are feeling and where you presently are. The next three steps will help you start to recognise and deal with your masks.

- Take a moment to ask yourself "Where am I? Is there anything I am struggling with at the moment?" and if it is not clear, ask God to help you. Also, note down what masks you identify with and why you might have put these masks on in the first place, throughout this process ask God to be with you and prompt you.
- Then throughout the next week, identify moments you mask your true feelings and thoughts and note these down. Can you identify a pattern or trigger?

- Once you have noticed what your masks are and the type of situations you use them in, begin to take small actions throughout the next few weeks to step outside the comfort zone of these masks when they come up, and ask Father God to be with you in this process.

- This may look like: relinquishing control over a situation or person; accepting an invite to an event you would usually have said no to; being open and honest with trusted people around you about how you're feeling instead of saying 'fine'. It could be telling yourself 'you are enough'; it could be reducing your use of sarcasm or lively personality to hide yourself; it could be trying to change your attitude to reflect positivity, rather than judgment or criticism.

To help you visualise letting go of these masks even more you can find some paper and write down what masks you have identified. Commit yourself to God again, then rip up the paper and throw it in the bin!

Let's be clear, this is not for any other reason than it's sometimes a good idea to make your body follow through with a decision your spirit has already made. Writing your mask down on a piece of paper and throwing it in the bin has no power whatsoever. The power is in the decision you are making to come out from behind your mask and dare to look into the mirror of God's Word barefaced, trusting Him with the rest.

Set aside time today, tomorrow or whenever you get the opportunity to reflect with God about the 'dressing room mirror' in your life. Use the Mirror Image Reflections cards if you want to dig a little deeper. My prayer is that you will have the courage to come from behind whatever you thought was protecting you and allow God to reveal the real you.

Prayer:

Father, thank you for revealing to me the masks that I have been hiding behind.

I don't want to live under a cycle of shame, fear and control any longer. I now give you complete access to every part of my heart and mind, allowing you to heal me of any of the past hurts and disappointments that have caused me to put those masks on in the first place.

I thank you that you have already given me the victory and that you are strengthening me daily as I walk in the truth of everything your Word promises for my future.

Help me to not fall back into the trap of these masks when challenges come my way, but to fix my eyes firmly on you, the Author and Perfecter of my faith, to show me who I am.

Lord, I thank you that with you all things are possible, that this is just the beginning, and that through ridding myself of every aspect of my identity that is not rooted in you, many more after me will be rescued also - family, friends, and those people you will connect me with who I don't even know yet. Thank you for all you have already done and are about to do.

In Jesus' name, Amen.

I KNOW THERE ARE THINGS You WANT TO CHANGE BUT You ARE loved JUST AS You ARE

Aimee Wood @bloommydear_

Chapter 2
Don't Look Back:
The Rear-View Mirror

––––––

Rear-view mirrors are essential when it comes to driving safely. We need to look behind us because it's important to understand and be aware of what's behind, in order to move forward safely.

Yet, if you were driving your car and were looking intently into the rear-view mirror for an extended period of time, sooner or later you would come to a standstill, either with a crash and a bang or because you'd become so engrossed with what was behind you; you'd have forgotten to keep your foot down.

When you look intently into the mirror of your past, your rear-view mirror, this is what you may see:
- Your **failures**
- Your **past hurts**
- Your **regrets**

Like ghosts from the past, the people who hurt you, the choices you made, the things you said and the things said to you echo endlessly in this reflection. Words, images and memories cut through your soul like sharp edged shards of glass from a broken mirror every time you let yourself spend too much time looking at this reflection.

We all have a past, we all have regrets and some of us have to spend time dealing with the painful consequences of things that have happened to us and around us. I am not devaluing or minimising the pain and the power of our past, but be warned, constantly looking behind will stop you moving forward safely. Only use the rear-view mirror as it's meant to be used - to inform you of what's behind you, in order to move forward safely.

Look Ahead, not Behind

The fact is, gazing into the rear-view mirror at the wrong moment can cause you to crash. Genesis 19 tells the story of Lot, his wife and their children. They lived in a place called Sodom, which God was going to destroy because of its wickedness. God told them to get out immediately or they would be swept away in the destruction of the city. Lot hesitated, so the angels that God had sent took him by the hand and led them out of the city.

Once they reached safety, one of the angels warned them to run for their lives without looking back and not to stop anywhere on the plains. They were clearly warned they would be swept away if they stopped to gaze in their rear-view mirror. God had prepared a safe place for them in the mountains, but despite this, Lot begged the angels to let him and his family stay closer to Sodom. So the angels let them take refuge in a small village nearby.

You would think that Lot and his wife would have been glad to leave the evil and wickedness of Sodom behind and step into the new future God had provided for them. But unfortunately Lot's wife hesitated; she disobeyed what the angels had said and looked back instead of focusing on what lay ahead. It was a costly mistake and she paid for that backwards glance into her rear-view mirror with her life.

When God says it's time to move on, we can become hesitant like Lot was. There is a grace and an understanding for this, as this story shows. God will take us by the hand and lead us just as the angel did with Lot. He will lead us through the process of escaping our past and into a new future. For some, this journey will not be an easy one. It will require forgiveness, determination and wisdom from people you trust, but as long as you are moving forward and keeping your hand in His, He will, through His grace and mercy, still rescue us.

Sometimes, as part of dealing with our past, we have to look back in order to set things right. We might have to forgive those who hurt us, we might need counselling or therapy to work through some of the issues from our past. That's okay for a season, but for everyone without exception, there will come a time when God draws a line and asks you to move on. To let it go and trust Him with your future by letting go of your past.

Setting the Pace

___

God wants to lead us on a journey which takes us from our past and into our future. He wants to get some momentum going in our lives to get us moving in the right direction, yet He allows us to set the pace. When Lot said that he wanted to flee to a village that was closer to Sodom, God allowed this. It wasn't God's first choice but He allowed Lot to take smaller steps to his freedom, as long as he did not stop moving and did not look back.

The same goes for us. **Never be afraid that God will make you deal with your past at a rate you are not able to sustain.** God can (and sometimes does) bring emotional healing in an instant but very often he will go at the pace we set. Sometimes we need to get counselling and talk through the painful issues from our past with a professional or someone we trust. Sometimes a person will need to find expert help such as the support we provide at Mercy UK, but whatever the journey from your past into your future looks like, there is one common denominator for all.

There will come a moment when God asks us to let go, to leave it all behind, to no longer identify with who we were, what we did, or what was done to us in the past. Instead, we must embrace the amazing future He has planned through the power of forgiveness.

Lot's wife struggled to let go of the past. She probably had family, friends, a job; her whole life was in that place, but God called her out of it because there was no future for her there. Yet she did not trust Him; she clung to her past and it cost her everything - her hopes, her dreams, her potential, her chance of freedom and ultimately, her life.

When we decide to look in the rear-view mirror and allow the past to dominate our outlook, it can also cause the death of our hopes, dreams and potential. Don't make the same mistake. Don't fear letting go of the past. Trust that God is taking you to a new future and will lead you to a place of safety.

God's Mirror will Release You into Your Future, not Trap You in Your Past

I remember as a child going to the circus and watching in awe as the trapeze artist moved with grace and courage through the air - to me it looked like she was flying. At just the right moment, seconds before gravity would demand its price, her hands grabbed the next trapeze and she would fly again.

I imagine the most frightening moment for the trapeze artist must be when she has to let go of the trapeze she is holding onto. The timing has to be perfect and she must not fear the moment where she is left empty handed: for without letting go of one, she cannot take hold of the other. It would be a poor show if all the crowd could see was a person clinging onto a trapeze for dear life, refusing to let go and so ending up swinging aimlessly back and forth until she gradually slowed down to a stop.

Yet many of us live our lives like that. We swing back and forth giving the impression to all who watch that there is in fact motion in our lives when, all the while, we are simply covering the same ground over and over again. We remain stuck in the same place because we refuse to let go and trust God to catch us.

The excitement, the adrenalin, the very purpose of being a trapeze artist is to fly, to soar, to feel the air all around and then to safely grab the trapeze that swings into your line of sight just in time to take you to the next one.

Moving forward will always require you to let go of the past and trust that God will help you grab what's coming with both hands. It's not enough to release just one hand from the bar. You can't hold on to your past and grasp your future at the same time. If you try to hold onto both trapezes, you will find yourself in conflict, under pressure, and left dangling in a very uncomfortable position.

God will always fill your empty space; he is drawn to it. The trouble is most of us are so full of the things we refuse to let go of that there's no space left for God to fill. We fear the emptiness of that space. We fear who we will be when the past no longer defines us. We don't trust God with our future and so we choose to look back and that mirror traps us again.

Jeremiah 29:11 (NIV)

"For I know the plans I have for you," says the Lord, "plans to prosper you and not to harm you, plans to give you hope and future." God has a future planned for us. It is a future where we have the strength to help others, where our issues are no longer holding us captive. But all the things we dream of, the plans we have, the longing for purpose, meaning and usefulness in our lives, will be ours only when we dare to let go of the things that are trapping us in our past.

Jeremiah 29:11 (NIV)

Turning Remorse into Resolve

There comes a point when we have to decide that enough is enough and we choose to stop sabotaging our future by gazing at the past. I call it 'turning remorse into resolve'. In the Collins English Dictionary the word 'remorse' means 'a sense of deep regret and guilt'. It comes from the Latin word 'remorsus' which means 'a gnawing inside.'

This is such an accurate description of the turmoil caused in our lives when we continue to gaze at a mirror image distorted by the past. It can create a gnawing sensation of being trapped by guilt, shame, fear, despair and hopelessness day after day. But 'resolve' on the other hand, means this: 'to decide or determine firmly, to change, alter, to make up the mind of; cause or decide, to find the answer or solution, to bring to an end, a firmness of purpose and determination'.

To me, 'resolve' describes what it looks like to take your eyes off the rear-view mirror and fix it firmly ahead. Having resolve will result in change, and give you a 'whatever it takes' attitude to being transformed and made whole: to be released from the trap of the past.

This changing remorse into resolve is something we have been privileged to witness in the lives of so many young women who have been through the Mercy UK programme.

Kirsten, one of our beautiful graduates said,

'My life before Mercy UK is best described as hopeless; always striving for happiness and love, perfection and control, but never being able to attain any of it. I spent so much of my life trying to fix everything including myself, but the more I tried the more out of control everything got; till eventually I gave up trying.

I allowed the depression and addictions that were controlling my life to overtake me.

Then I came to a point in my life where I had enough. Mercy was literally my last hope. I knew that this had to work. I knew that things had to change; that I had to change. I had tried it every other way, now I had to try it God's way.'

That is what turning 'remorse' into 'resolve' looks like. There is a reason why the rear-view mirror is so small, it's only meant for the odd glance, to help you set your course forward.

The Key that Unlocks the Door

Sometimes we can feel trapped by our past. It's like being locked in a room where the smallest thing can bring back a memory that triggers feelings of anger, hurt, betrayal and rejection, so we bang on the door screaming to be let out. We get angry at the people who put us in that room and we demand to be let out. But we have the key in our hands all along - we just don't realise it.

The key that can unlock the prison of your past and set you free is forgiveness. Without forgiveness, true freedom is impossible. Without forgiveness, we will remain locked in that room. Unless you learn to forgive, the door to your future will stay firmly locked and you will remain a prisoner of your past. These are strong words but Jesus was very clear about the need for forgiveness.

Matthew 6:15 (NIV)

"But if you do not forgive others their sins, your Father will not forgive your sins."

Matthew 6:15 (NIV)

Forgiveness is a choice to begin a process that may take time. **Forgiveness rarely comes from feelings. In fact, our feelings will often work against us. It requires an act of your will, an act of obedience to God's will.** Right feelings will (eventually) follow right actions and as you act on the decision to forgive, the feelings will follow. If you ask Him to help you, I can guarantee you He will!

Perhaps you have been the victim of unspeakable pain, hurt, betrayal or abuse. Maybe you can't even remember a time when you haven't been mistreated or misunderstood in some way. These kinds of events can make us feel justified to live in unforgiveness. These things seem too painful to forgive; you feel that your resentment and hatred of the people that hurt you is deserved. You may think, 'Surely if I forgive such devastating trespasses, it's like excusing them or accepting that what they did was okay?' But this isn't how forgiveness works. Forgiveness fully accepts and acknowledges the hurt and pain that has been caused. It does not belittle it, nor does it justify the behaviour of those who hurt you. Instead, it chooses to take the burden of judgement from your back and places it onto Jesus'.

Dead Man Walking

───

I once asked God to help me explain the damage unforgiveness can cause and he showed me a picture of a person walking along a road with a corpse on their back. It was rotting with a foul stench and toxic fumes radiating from it. The person carrying the corpse was unaware of the smell, she couldn't see the poison from the corpse seeping into the friction burns its weight had caused on her back. She walked along, burdened by the weight of her unforgiveness with anger propelling her forward and pain causing her to stumble every now and then.

Friends would walk alongside to try and tell the person about the corpse, but she didn't trust anyone enough to listen. Instead, she would scowl to chase them off, or smile sweetly to make them think she had heard them while the corpse continued to infect her.

Then I saw God handing the person a huge pair of scissors with 'choose to forgive' written on them. As she took the scissors and began the process of forgiveness, I saw each cord binding her to the corpse cut and it begin to fall away. Once each cord was loose, I saw God take the corpse from her back and place it onto Jesus' back. Forgiveness equals freedom from a rotting burden that is not yours to carry.

Romans 12:19 (MSG)

'Don't insist on getting even; that's not for you to do. "I'll do the judging," says God. "I'll take care of it. "'

Romans 12:19 (MSG)

Dealing with Consequences

Forgiveness is not saying that what happened is justifiable - it is handing it over for God's justice to work in place of our own judgements. It is not our place to take responsibility for what others have done, we are only responsible for our own choices which means that with the choice to forgive, we also have the choice and the right to assert boundaries.

Boundaries determine worth. If something isn't worth anything, why protect it? It's the reason we put our jewellery safe in a box, or have a fence around our gardens - these things represent boundaries, which signify something of worth.

Worth is set according to the price someone is willing to pay and the Truth is, your worth was set when Jesus offered His life for you. You are of great worth and therefore, it is your responsibility not only to forgive but also to protect your life through developing healthy boundaries.

Sometimes this means saying 'no' to someone who is an unhealthy influence on you or who requires more time or resource from you than you are willing to offer. Sometimes, having boundaries means upholding consequences such as separating yourself from a relationship which is hurtful or abusive, or no longer lending your friend the money or sharing personal information which seems to become gossip. You may forgive someone for the hurt their choices may have had on you but it is not your responsibility to remove their consequences. Forgiveness is a result of your choice; consequence is a result of their choice.

Consequences are a healthy part of building relationships and navigating through life's challenges. You will find that when you uphold consequences and assert boundaries, your relationships flourish as expectations and needs are met in a healthy way, simply because it becomes clear where you end and somebody else begins.

If you are in a situation where you are at risk of getting hurt, of exploitation or of control and coercion in any form, put in boundaries and practical strategies that ensure your contact with that person is minimal and that you have the support you need to assert some boundaries or break away from the relationship. Speak to a trusted friend or email our support services for advice.

Nostalgia: the Rose-tinted Glasses

It's not just negative experiences that can keep us trapped in the past. Sometimes, we need to make a decision not to fill our minds with nostalgia. Nostalgia is defined in the Collins English dictionary as 'yearning for the return of past circumstances' or in other words, seeing the past through rose-tinted glasses.

Nostalgia is not a friend. It can distort our memories and leave us trying to reproduce or somehow relive good times again. Sometimes it's because those past times were indeed good but often times it's because the rose-tinted glasses are causing us to put a 'feel-good filter' on those memories.

It's a dangerous filter. It can cause us to fear the future, to resent our present or to long for a past that seemed so good, even if in reality it wasn't. I have spoken to so many women coming out of a difficult, even abusive relationship who in the midst of the pain found the courage to leave, to draw a line and say: 'no more.' Yet, a few weeks later, they look back with fondness and nostalgia wishing they were back with him. They allow nostalgia to amplify the good and minimise the bad and too often it has caused them to return to a relationship or situation that should have and could have ended.

The Israelites suffered from this rose-tinted perspective of the rear view mirror. Only six weeks after being miraculouly delivered from centuries of slavery and abuse, they began to grumble and complain about the present and to doubt the future God had promised. Exodus 16 tells us:

- The whole Israelite community set out from Elim and came to the Desert of Sin, which is between Elim and Sinai, on the fifteenth day of the second month after they had come out of Egypt.

- In the desert the whole community grumbled against Moses and Aaron. The Israelites said to them, "If only we had died by the LORD's hand in Egypt! There we sat around pots of meat and ate all the food we wanted, but you have brought us out into this desert to starve this entire assembly to death."

Can you spot the rose-tinted reflection of nostalgia in their words? They are fondly remembering the food in their bellies but in doing so forgetting the whip on their backs and the chains on their feet.

Having a rear-view mirror is useful; essential even. A quick glance in it lets us know it is safe to move forward but we must ensure that we don't allow it to distract us from the road ahead.

Looking back during a time when God has called you forward is dangerous - like staring intently into the rear-view mirror of your car. You will stop, you will crash, you will hinder your progress and it can cost you your future. We cannot turn back time, our focus should be ahead not behind. However good or bad behind us looks, it is merely meant to be glanced at.

Another Mercy UK graduate, Sarah, wrote these words:

"Mercy helped me to recognise how to put my past fears and failures behind me and how they do not define me. I am not a product of my past. Throughout my journey at Mercy I realised that all my life I have been believing the lies that told me I was useless, I was worthless, I was stupid, ugly and not wanted. I finished Mercy knowing who I am in Christ. I am chosen, I'm accepted, I am treasured, I am loved, unique and special to my Heavenly Father."

Let's get practical
Leaving offense in the past

———

As I said before, forgiveness is the key to not letting your rear view mirror show you a false reflection and distract you from the direction you are heading in. So, it's time to not just think about forgiving people, but to bite the bullet and start the forgiving process. Take a moment to get a piece of paper - this is your forgiveness list. This list could go back 20 seconds or 20 years, it could range from the smallest wrong doing, to things that seem to be unforgivable. This list might be short, it might be as long as your arm. While you are writing names, take a minute to ask God if there's anyone you've forgotten, if there's anyone you didn't actually know is still causing you offense and make sure you pop them down on your list.

Once you have got your list - don't worry if it looks daunting, having it written down visually can help you to process it. Now, go through the list with each name, and here is a little prayer to help you.

Father,
I forgive _____ for _____ . I ask that you help me move
forward from this offense, and I pray that you will bless them.
In Jesus' name, Amen.

You may need to pray this prayer once, you may need to pray it 1000 times, you might need to pray it when you get angry, when you wake up in the morning or simply whenever you see or think about the person. But this prayer will help you through the process of forgiveness, it is often not a 'snap-your-fingers and you no longer have to deal with forgiving them' situation. But one day, maybe after saying this prayer twice or many times, you will look back and not have to say it anymore, the process will be complete.

Prayer:

Father, I come before you now and ask that you would help me. Help me to be free from all that has happened to me; all the pain, the despair and the tormenting thoughts that go round and round.

Lord, I pray that you would make a way where there seems to be no way. I pray that you would take me by the hand and lead me out from the place that represents destruction and disaster.

Thank you for the cross. I ask that you forgive me for staying here in this place so long. I don't want to be trapped by this mirror any more.

I choose to believe what your Word says about me. I choose to believe that you know the plans you have for me, plans to prosper me and not to harm me, plans to give me a hope and a future.

Thank you that as I work in partnership with your Holy Spirit, as I look within myself and turn remorse into resolve, I will walk away from the destruction that is behind and into the future you have planned and prepared for me.

In Jesus' name, Amen.

Chapter 3
Self-esteem or God-esteem:
The Full-Length Mirror

Most of us have a full-length mirror in the house somewhere. This mirror helps us check if we are fit to be seen in public. "Am I showing them the best version of me? Does this top go with these trousers; do I look the right size in this outfit? Should I wear the black shoes or the brown boots?"

This 'full-length mirror' represents our self-image - our sense of worth and value. The reflection we see in this mirror will determine whether we feel we are presentable and acceptable to those around us.

When we look intently into this mirror, it can whisper untruths into our lives. It tells us that we are worthless, not up to standard and unacceptable. This mirror lies to us about the importance of our shape, our weight, our image and can undermine our sense of worth and confidence. We will only see what we think people think of us, what they have said to us, or what we imagine they are saying about us.

Our sense of self will become heavily based on the opinions of those around us and it'll change every day. We don't know who we are because our identity is caught up in other people's opinions of us and this mirror will trap us here, if we let it.

The tell-tale signs of this mirror's presence in our lives is clear: we build ourselves up when others like us or approve of us and we beat ourselves up when they don't.

When a compliment comes our way, it's like food; we can feed on it for days. The comment gets mulled over and over again and our self-esteem will be built on such positive comments. But heaven forbid if someone should say something bad, or even worse, ignore us, block us or unfriend us. Why didn't they like my picture? Why wasn't I invited? Have I upset them? What if they don't like me anymore?

What if they tell their friends what they really think of me and then none of them will like me anymore? Is this top I'm wearing the right label, the right colour? Will this new hair colour look good on my social media?

This mirror will influence everything you think about yourself, it will be your harshest critic and it is merciless. It will tell you that you fall short of people's expectations and it will leave you feeling under-valued, worthless and low: a failure, a reject.

At Mercy, we see the symptoms of hurt and broken lives every day: eating disorders, self harm, suicidal ideation and the anguish that comes from years of abuse.

But underneath all of those big branches of dysfunction lie roots that are giving life to those behaviours. It might surprise you to learn that a common root cause of these problems is low self-esteem; an intense lack of value and worth.

Though not everyone who suffers from low self-esteem has tried to commit suicide and not everyone self-harms or has depression, the symptoms of low self-esteem reach beyond the confines of the young women we support through the Mercy UK programme - poor self-image, low sense of worth and value is all around us in womanhood.

It's present in a woman's constant need to compare herself to others; it's present in our need to gossip about those around us and in our obsession with weight and diets to fit the accepted standard set by our society.

A quick look on any magazine shelf or online blog will tell you that our appetite for gossip and beauty tips is insatiable. A quick click online will show you millions watching YouTube videos on how to look like everyone else. These are all symptoms of an entire generation being trapped by the lies told by our full length mirror of worth and value.

Opening our Eyes

——

One of our beautiful and brave young women had believed the lies of the full-length mirror for so long that she no longer even saw her image reflected as it truly was. Instead, when she looked in the mirror, she obsessed over her size and was utterly convinced that she was grotesquely overweight. When she looked in the mirror she will tell you that she saw rolls of unhealthy fat spill over her hips and stomach and legs. She dressed in over-sized clothes to hide what she believed was an over-sized body. The reality is, she was not overweight - not at all, but no-one could tell her otherwise, not even the mirror.

One day, her facilitator lay out rolls of paper which practically covered the whole floor! She marked the young woman's height in the middle and told her that this indicated the top of her head and the tips of her toes. She then handed the resident a marker pen and encouraged her to draw out what she believed was her body's outline. The resident drew what she saw reflected in the mirror every day - someone she believed to be obese.

The facilitator then took the marker pen and asked if the resident was willing to have her true outline drawn. The brave resident agreed, took a breath and lay down on the paper. The facilitator drew around her body, asking the resident to notice at all times that the pen was giving a true outline. As the resident stood and turned to look at the outline her jaw dropped and her eyes widened.

She shook her head, repeating, 'Is that me? Is that me?' She wrestled for a moment with what she saw, but being unable to deny what had just taken place, the lies that the distorted mirror image had fed her fell like scales from her eyes and she was able to see her true frame for the very first time.

The resident reported being able to see an honest reflection in the mirror from that point and although she knew she still had a healing journey ahead of her, she realised that if this had been a lie all along, then what else had the world led her to believe about her self-worth and self-image?

And this is where the journey starts - being willing to open our eyes to an honest reflection, not just an honest reflection of what we see in the mirror without judgement, criticism or shame, but an honest reflection of what we believe to be 'real beauty'.

Is Beauty only Skin Deep?

Dove, one of Unilever's largest beauty brands, commissioned a report called 'The Real Truth About Beauty: A Global Report' to try to have a better understanding of the whole concept women have about beauty and its relationship with how we feel about ourselves.

The key findings are fascinating:

Just 4% of women around the world consider themselves beautiful.

4%

11% of girls globally are comfortable describing themselves as 'beautiful'.

11%

72% of girls feel tremendous pressure to be beautiful.

72%

More than half of women globally (54%) agree that when it comes to how they look, they are their own worst beauty critic.

54%

80% of women agree that every woman has something about her that is beautiful, but do not see their own beauty.

80%

Surprised by this result, the researchers looked into the definition of beauty that most women had responded to and found that they were defining the word 'beautiful' only in terms of physical beauty.

It shows that we have totally bought into the concept that beauty is only physical appearance and nothing else. So, when asked if they thought they were 'beautiful', it is no surprise that 96% of women said no.

In support of this research, a more recent study by the Royal Society of Public Health found that body image is still an issue for many young people, but in particular females in their teenage years and early twenties. This study found, again, more shocking results that as many as nine in ten teenage girls admit that they are unhappy with their body.

This distorted mirror image tells us that being 'physically attractive' (defined according to strict criteria that few actually meet) equals feeling acceptable to society, which in turn equals happiness, fulfilment and contentment.

Conversely, not feeling beautiful (so 96% of us) equals unacceptable to society, which equals unhappiness, discontent and unfulfillment.

Being accepted by those around us is a basic need; we all want to find acceptance, but this will only happen in a healthy way when we have accepted ourselves first. This is by looking into God's mirror and choosing to accept the image He presents to us, not by measuring ourselves according to what our society tells us we should look like.

We will never be able to control what people think or say about us, or to us. Many of us have been hurt by words spoken in anger, spitefulness or jealousy towards us.

But those words do not have the power to change who we are or how we behave unless we give them the power to do so. The moment we attach worth to what that person has said above what God has said about us, is the moment we give those words the power to destroy us.

Reinhard Bonnke, a prominent Christian speaker and evangelist said, *"If you value the praise of man, then the criticism of man will destroy you. Seek the honour of God, not the approval of man."*

It came as a huge shock to me when I discovered that I had been caught by this mirror after I had my first baby.

Before my pregnancy, I was confident in my body and the way I looked. I did not realise how much of my confidence was built on that temporary state, instead of on knowing who I was in God and what He thought of me.

After my son was born and my body changed significantly, I suddenly became aware of my lack of confidence. I became self conscious about walking into a room full of (in my opinion) slim and attractive women. I hid my shape away in baggy clothes and mourned the loss of my prime (at only 26 years old!).

I envied those who seemed to lose their 'baby weight' in minutes while I went on faddy diets and crazy exercise routines to lose it. I had always been naturally slim and felt that everyone was watching my weight to see if I would return to my previous shape and size.

This was not helped by a comment made by an acquaintance shortly after I had my baby. 'What happened to you!?' he asked. 'You used to be so beautiful, now you look like... well, you know...'

He never finished the sentence, perhaps realising the mistake he had made, but the damage was done and my worst fears confirmed. I was no longer beautiful or attractive, which to me meant I was no longer acceptable and my confidence plummeted.

Under the Knife

My lowest point came when I sat in the office of a cosmetic surgeon discussing an operation to turn back time on my breasts and get rid of some of the extra skin my 10lb baby had left me with. We didn't have the money, but I was determined and was prepared to go into debt to try and regain what I felt I had lost.

I sat there while the surgeon told me the risks, which included anything from mild infection, to a seriously adverse reaction that could permanently disfigure me. Was I still happy to sign the disclaimer and pay the deposit on the small fortune it would cost?

I walked out of that room, feeling so confused, low and miserable. I asked God if having the surgery was ok. All he said to me was, "Does it really matter that much?" My initial response was, "Yes, it does actually", but I knew that God's question to me was an invitation for me to discover what it means to truly know that beauty is so much more than what your body looks like.

I am not against cosmetic surgery, but I believe that our motives for having it done really need to be examined. I have friends who have had it done and it was the right decision for them and I supported them in it. But it would have been the wrong choice for me.

Under the Needle

———

Back then, plastic surgery was a huge commitment - it was expensive and not easily accessible. It required a process that gave you time to think, which is what I needed to help me make an informed and thought through decision not to go ahead. Now, however, it's simply a matter of nipping round to the woman in the boutique down the road, and you can completely change the appearance of your face over a lunch-time appointment.

Again, there is no shame in doing this, but the ease and availability of this process takes away from the opportunity to consider it carefully. You will naturally consider something that costs thousands of pounds and may take weeks to recover from for longer and at a deeper level, than you would consider a half hour treatment that needs next to no recovery time, even though the implications can be just as permanent.

The action of doing this is not the problem, the motive behind it is. Fixing the outside will never fix the inside- it only ever works the other way around. That's what I had to learn.

So, you're considering cosmetic surgery or augmentation. How can you be sure this is the right decision for you?

Are you doing this for yourself, and not to please or impress anybody else?

NO → It's good to identify any external pressures or motivations for your decision. If it is to please or impress anybody else, then don't do it. Ask God to show you when you first believed surgery or augmentation was an option in order to be acceptable.

YES ↓

If you were to give your physical, emotional and mental health a score out of 0-10 for good health and resilience, would you score highly for each one?

NO → There is no way of predicting the impact of cosmetic surgery or augmentation on your physical, mental or emotional health. It's important that your body is in good health and that you have resilient emotional and mental health to adjust to any change or unexpected outcomes.

YES ↓

Do you have the finances available for the procedure and for any care required following it?

NO → Make sure this decision doesn't leave you financially short by saving up enough to not only pay for the procedure, but also for the aftercare.

YES ↓

Imagine you are giving a presentation about your decision, can you confidently explain the risks, the reasons you chose the practitioner and your personal expectations?

NO → Making an informed decision means understanding the risks, reviewing the prospective practitioner and setting realistic expectations. Consider each of these things in full, with trusted friends.

YES ↓

If someone were to ask you what God is saying about this decision, could you answer confidently?

NO → Knowing what God says is like having an anchor in a storm. Should the unexpected occur, you can hold on to what you know God said to you. By including God in the decision from the beginning, you can walk with Him, right to the end.

YES ↓

When you imagine yourself committing to the procedure, do you have a sense of inner peace?

NO → Peace guides and guards the heart in decision-making which is why we must pursue it and position ourselves in a place of peace before making any potentially life-changing decisions.

It sounds like you've thought and prayed this through. Feel free to get in touch with support services for any further support or prayer.

God used my experiences to reveal to me what the foundations of my self-esteem, confidence and sense of self-worth were built upon.

Having a positive body image isn't believing that your body looks good, it's knowing that your body is good - regardless of your looks. It's not about thinking you're beautiful, because what is beauty anyway? It's having a deep knowledge that you are more than beautiful. Your body is a vessel, not an ornament.

We all have a need to feel significant, to have a sense of security and acceptance. But whilst we try to find those things from any other source but Christ, we will be seeing our lives in this full length mirror of distortion.

The Cambridge dictionary defines self-esteem as *'a belief and confidence in one's own ability'.*

The fact is, there is something wrong with the very definition of 'self-esteem'.

We need a shift in thinking - we cannot be those who gain our sense of worth, value, identity and esteem from what we see in the mirror or what we hear people say about, or to us. We cannot meet the demands of life around us by relying on our own abilities, we must change the source from self-esteem to God-esteem.

Self-esteem cannot come from external sources, changing your sense of worth and value is not something that is done to you - it's an internal shift, a choice to look in the mirror of God's word, rather than the full length mirror of lies.

We need God-esteem - a belief that what God's mirror says over us is Truth and our esteem in God and His esteem in us is the very foundation of our worth and value.

Many of us base our sense of identity on what people have said or done to us or on the issues we have to deal with in life: disappointment, abuse, divorce, debt, bullies, loss. We allow that distorted full length mirror to speak and pull our self-image down into distortion.

It might not be your physical beauty that bothers you. Maybe for you it is people-pleasing and you only feel good about yourself when people like you. Or maybe it's compromising what you know is right because it doesn't fit in with the status quo. Perhaps your life is being ruled by the needs of others. Or maybe you hate yourself because the people who should have loved you didn't and your self-image was shaped by rough hands.

The fact is, even if every person who is supposed to love you does and even if you've never experienced abuse or hurt, your security and sense of value is still at risk if it's rooted in the wrong things. Even though I had a loving husband, a beautiful baby and great friends, their love did not protect me from an attack on my self image. Few are immune to this mirror of lies until they choose to shift their gaze and start to look at their true reflection in the mirror of God's word.

The very foundations that our lives are built on become unstable when we give power to lies instead of embracing the truth of what God has said. We build our lives on the sands of low self-esteem and worthlessness and the Bible tells us when our lives are built on sand, the storms of life will come and wipe us out.

Jesus told us to build our house on the Rock. Our lives, all thatflows out of us needs to have a firm foundation. That firm foundation is made up of a sense of identity in Christ, and a sense of worth and value based on the Word of Truth - and nothing else.

He will begin to change us from the inside out; he will start to make sure that we are building on the Rock by speaking to us about our true value and worth.

God's Mirror Will Show You Your True Value
—

Jesus tells us in John 8:32 (NIV) that the Truth will set you free. This is a commonly quoted scripture but often without the context. Jesus actually says: "And you shall know the Truth and the Truth will set you free."

Therefore, it's not simply the Truth that sets you free; it's the Truth you know that sets you free. And how else will you know the Truth than to read the source of Truth – the Word of God? How else will you know the Truth other th**an to know Him who is the Truth? How else will you know acceptance, worth,** value and identity if not in the mirror of God's Word?

God's mirror works in direct contrast to the false reflection of the 'full length' mirror. His mirror will teach us that our sense of significance and value comes from understanding that we can never increase or decrease in value to God. It is set, not by who we are or what we do, but by who God is and what Christ did for us.

Value is established by how much someone is willing to pay - and Jesus paid with His life. Our worth and value is non-negotiable, we can't enter into discussion with God about worth, it is set not by who we are or what we have done but by who He is and what He has done for us.

God's mirror, His Word, will tell us exactly what we are worth and how loved we are. It's reflection is clear, unchanging and not dependent on whether we think we deserve it or not.

God's Word is very clear about our beauty, our value and our worth. Just to prove my point, let me 'scripture blast' you.

_____ *Jeremiah 1:5 (NIV)*

Before I formed you in the womb, I knew you, before you were born I set you apart.

Jeremiah 1:5 (NIV) _____

_____ *Exodus 19:5 (AMPC)*

Now therefore, if you will listen to My voice in truth and keep My covenant, then you shall be My own special treasure from among and above all peoples; for all the earth is Mine.

Exodus 19:5 (AMPC) _____

_____ *Psalm 139 (MSG)*

Oh yes, you shaped me first inside, then out; you formed me in my mother's womb. I thank you, High God—you're breathtaking! Body and soul, I am marvelously made! I worship in adoration— what a creation! You know me inside and out, you know every bone in my body; You know exactly how I was made, bit by bit, how I was sculpted from nothing into something. Like an open book, you watched me grow from conception to birth; all the stages of my life were spread out before you, The days of my life all prepared before I'd even lived one day.

Psalm 139 (MSG) _____

_____ *Ephesians 1:11 (NIV)*

In him we were also chosen, having been predestined according to the plan of him who works out everything in conformity with the purpose of his will.

Ephesians 1:11 (NIV) _____

The Lord did not choose you and lavish His love on you because you were larger or greater than any other nations, for you were the smallest of all nations. It was simply because the Lord loves you.

Deuteronomy 7:7-8 (NLT)

I'll call nobodies and make them somebodies. I'll call the unloved and make them beloved.

Romans 9:25 (MSG)

Long before he laid down earth's foundations, he had us in mind, had settled on us as the focus of his love, to be made whole and holy by his love. Long, long ago he decided to adopt us into his family through Jesus Christ (what pleasure he took in planning this!).

Ephesians 1:3-5 (NIV)

I think these scriptures clearly show we are the focus of His love; He personally created and knit us together and He doesn't just think we look beautiful, He thinks we are beautiful.

Long before we ever lived, he planned to adopt us into His family through Jesus' death and resurrection. He decided to pay the ultimate price so that we could be His. He saw us. He saw our faces and thought we were worth it. Our value is set.

Our sense of value can be eroded: by ourselves, by others' words, actions and neglect or by the guilt we feel from the things we have done. But God has determined that our own perception of our worth doesn't change our value to Him.

There's an old illustration that demonstrates this concept beautifully. Imagine that I offered you a £50 note. You would want to accept it because it's valuable. It's worth £50 exactly, no more or no less.

But before I handed it over, I told you that this £50 had a past. It had been used to pay for sex with a prostitute. It was stolen from a man who was beaten and his blood was still on it. It had been rolled up and had drugs sniffed through it and had spent many years hidden under a mattress forgotten by the one who owned it. It's torn, stained and still has all the residue of filth stuck on it from the awful ways it had been used in the past.

Would you still want it? Of course you would, but why? The fact is: it's still worth £50 no matter what is has been used for because its value is set by its maker. Its value is not determined by what has happened to it, what it looks like or how it feels.

God didn't use our imperfections to negotiate a lower price. He paid in full; one Son, one price, one value. He paid the same for you as He did for the most holy and perfect person you can think of. Our worth to God is non-negotiable.

God doesn't love us because we are valuable; we are valuable because He loves us.

Let's get Practical
Putting on Your Armour

——

We need to guard our hearts from the distorted reflections of the full-length mirror and it's the armour of God that is our protection and needs to be part of our everyday wardrobe. This armour will help us to see our true reflection with no interference from others. Ephesians 6:12 (NIV) tells us what this armour looks like.

"For our struggle is not against flesh and blood, but against the rulers, against the authorities, against the powers of this dark world and against the spiritual forces of evil in the heavenly realms. Therefore put on the full armor of God, so that when the day of evil comes, you may be able to stand your ground, and after you have done everything, to stand. Stand firm then, with the belt of truth buckled around your waist, with the breastplate of righteousness in place, and with your feet fitted with the readiness that comes from the gospel of peace. In addition to all this, take up the shield of faith, with which you can extinguish all the flaming arrows of the evil one. Take the helmet of salvation and the sword of the Spirit, which is the word of God."

Ephesians 6:12 (NIV)

A good way of putting your armour on is to make a visual list of it and place it somewhere you will see it every morning. Put this list of the armour of God above your bed, or on your bedside table, or near a desk you may sit at everyday, and the armour will remain present in your mind as your God-given protection.

Prayer:
Father, I thank You for creating me and giving me life. Thank you that You loved me enough to send Your Son to die for me.

Lord, forgive me for not being in agreement with Your Word about my worth and value. Forgive me for being more concerned with what people think than what You think. From today, I choose to start renewing my mind and bringing it into alignment with what Your thoughts are regarding me.

Help me, Holy Spirit, to clearly see the lies I have believed about myself. Help me to see the Truth about my identity and worth as I look into the mirror of Your Word.

In Jesus' name, Amen.

AND AT
LAST, AFTER
YEARS
OF HATRED,
SHE BEGAN
TO
FINALLY
MAKE
PEACE
WITH
HERSELF

Aimee Wood @bloommydear_

Chapter 4
Who's The Fairest of Them All?
The Dance Studio Mirror

———

It was the first time I'd ever been in a dance studio - watching whilst a group of sweaty dancers rehearsed the same steps again and again, to the sound of a piano and the voice of a teacher shouting correction and encouragement in equal measures. My friend Fi was in the rehearsal, bending, turning, jumping and getting ready for that evening's performance. She had been a ballerina for years and was used to facing the rigorous demands of the dance studio mirror.

At the end of the rehearsal, I remember asking her what it was like to have to look at herself in the mirror all day. She looked at me for a moment and then made a profound statement: 'Actually, it's not looking at myself in the mirror that is difficult, it's looking at myself compared to everyone else that is the hardest part.'

And so I present to you the 'dance studio mirror'. This mirror is all about our lives and ourselves in comparison to those around us. This mirror will show us a false reflection of our identity- one defined by our performance compared to others.

It's an unfortunate trait us humans have: to compare ourselves to those around us, and usually we mark ourselves down. We feel depressed because everyone else has managed to get their grades, go to the right University, lose their pregnancy weight, organise their children's birthday party, get a great job, keep their house spotless and the list goes on.

We look in the dance studio mirror and watch everyone else's work-out. We see how competent they look compared to us.

They seem to be far more graceful in how they handle life; they look more together than us, more attractive than us. As we allow comparison to invade our life we feel under pressure because everyone else's show seems much more impressive than ours.

What we seldom realise is that those we compare ourselves to are also looking at us and feeling inadequate in exactly the same way. None of this is helped by the dance studio mirror's greatest ally, found on the flip side of our mobile phones - the selfie mirror.

A Filtered Reality

When you take a selfie, how many do you take? 1, 3 or maybe 55, or more? Do you upload it to an app which makes the bags under your eyes disappear? Do you pop a filter on it that makes your teeth whiter and your skin look flawless?

I'm not saying we shouldn't edit photos if we want to but how many of us edit our own photos flawlessly, caption them to show people what a good time we are having and then look at other people's social media, thinking that this is real life?

How many of us upload a holiday snap, well aware we are in our car in the pouring rain outside work, yet we are convinced that the girl we follow on Instagram is constantly on holiday in the sun, and that she's probably never had a miserable day in her life? Even if we ourselves have just spent 25 minutes making our picture look like the best version of our reality, we assume that the rest of the world is bringing their unfiltered, everyday routine to the table?

This little camera, this tiny mirror we carry around with us on a small screen is one that we can become entirely immersed in.

Whilst telling us we can see the whole world, this mirror fails to tell us we are seeing the whole world through a filter. Our viewpoint becomes shaped by Snapchat filters, Instagram stories, YouTube videos and Facebook updates - all of them adding another piece to the dance studio mirror of comparison. We can see ourselves and we can see others - lots of others! Except it's not a true reflection. It is a skewed perception of reality, and whether looking at ourselves in this mirror or others - comparison is a dangerous game.

The Dangers of the Unattainable

——

As we explored in the previous chapter, the temptation to find our worth and value by trying to fit in to the culture around us is immense. Social media bombards us with images of girls with lip fillers, cheek highlights, botox and lash extensions in their pyjamas, with the caption 'just woke up like this!' We forget the context by directly comparing ourselves to an idea that is a filtered, unattainable version of reality. When we start comparing ourselves with strangers on social media without any context of their actual reality, we risk doing serious damage to our own sense of self-confidence.

Studies have shown that when young girls and women in their teens and early twenties view Facebook for only a short period of time, their body image concerns are higher compared to individuals who do not use Facebook. Another study also demonstrated that women express a heightened desire to change their appearance such as face, hair and skin after spending time on Facebook.

Therefore, we need to be aware of what we are exposed to and what attitude we take towards what we see.

SOCIAL MEDIA

Research has
shown that
Instagram
has negative
effects on:

- **Anxiety**
- **Depression**
- **Loneliness**
- **Bullying**
- **Sleep**
- **Body Image**

The Power of Perspective

The power of perspective is imperative. The content of social media is not always the problem, it is sometimes how we look at it. To be informed, secure, free and know how much you are loved by the creator of the universe is an amazing perspective to have. Because as amazing as their life looks, you will know that your own life has a purpose and a plan, and you will know that the person you are looking at, just like everyone else, goes through their own highs and lows.

The wicked stepmother in the fairytale 'Snow White' didn't have social media, but she had the same weakness. Looking into the mirror of comparison led to insecurity and jealousy, and eventually her jealousy led her to destruction. In the same way, many people look into the dance studio mirror and ask, 'Mirror, mirror on the wall, who is the fairest, richest, most successful, best dressed, most spiritual, most generous, kindest, has the most likes and followers of them all? Is it me, or is it her?

The dance studio mirror will always show you an image of yourself that doesn't match up to those around. It will erode your sense of self-worth and confidence by making you feel you don't measure up as you constantly compare yourself to others.

Before I had children, I was a school teacher, earning a good salary and having the enviable status of 'professional'. Once I had my first baby, however, I realised that staying at home with my child had seriously affected the value others placed on my contribution to society.

I remember during this time applying for car insurance online and as I filled out the required information, I came to the box that asked for my occupation. As I was no longer teaching I scrolled down the list of options of professions that my car insurance company validated as legitimate, until I came to a sudden halt at 'housewife - no occupation'.

As I grudgingly selected this option, I came to the sad realisation that my status had dropped in our society's viewpoint to 'just a housewife' and I found that it caused a pressure to conform within me, to 'be someone' and 'do something' and it began to erode my sense of identity. I was looking in the wrong mirror.

This dance studio mirror will tell us that we need to perform; to match up to the standards people have set for us, we must become all that 'they' expect us to become. However, we should never find our worth in a status, job title or in how society views us. We need to realise that when God looks at us, he sees only us. He made each of us unique, therefore nothing and no-one compares to you!

God's Mirror Reflection Shows Only You

——

There are some verses in Galatians which I love because they describe God's true reflection of us.

——————————————————————————— *Galatians 6:4-5 (MSG)*

"Make a careful exploration of who you are and the work you have been given, and then sink yourself into that. Don't be impressed with yourself. Don't compare yourself with others. Each of you must take responsibility for doing the creative best you can with your own life."

Galatians 6:4-5 (MSG) ————————————————————————

This is such a freedom bringing scripture. It says 'you have to do the creative best with your own life.' That means you have to do your best, not be the best!

You don't have to be better than anyone else - you can just be you. Nothing you do for God will be compared to what others have done for Him, He just sees you in relation to you. How liberating it is to realise you are in a one-woman race!

This Truth releases us to help others, because when there is no need to compare, we are no longer threatened by or jealous of them. When we stop being in competition we release one another to be the person God is shaping us to be. When we have a clear understanding of our own test, our own tasks, and our own callings, it gives a confidence that comes from knowing who we are in Christ - a Godly confidence that isn't dependent on the opinions of others.

Comparison creates insecurity; it feeds a lack of confidence in ourselves and makes us question our own identity and relationship with God.

Heulwen, one of the Mercy graduates, said this about it:

God taught me on my Mercy journey that I'd been looking at myself through the wrong lenses. I'd been looking at myself through the lens of comparison. I'd been looking at myself through the lens of self-hatred and disgust. I'd been looking at myself through the lens of unworthiness. I'd been looking at myself through the lens of not-good-enough. Unwanted. Stupid. Insert more negative lenses here and you get the picture. But He didn't leave it there. He showed me where I'd picked up these lenses and gently but surely helped me put them back down until there was only one lens left that I had covered the whole time - the lens of Jesus. He showed me that through Christ I am whole, I am loved, I am redeemed, I am more than enough, more than my fears, more than my past and more than any untruthful lens I could ever look through. My identity is in Him alone - I am made in the wondrous image of God. And that, quite honestly, is the most precious lesson I could have ever learnt.

Another Mercy graduate, Laura, tells a story of her experience of comparison;

The year is 2007, it's a summer's day, and I'm about to receive my dissertation results - ten months of researching, drafting, redrafting - all comes down to this one minute. And I've worked it out, all I need is 55, 55 marks and I get a 2:1 overall in my degree, the one thing I've been working towards for three years, so you can imagine, the anxiety, the anticipation as I turn the page over. But there it is, top right hand corner 58... I had done it. I had achieved the thing I had been working towards for three years, and I was starting to feel proud of myself. But now that I had my result I was kind of eager to find out how my friend had done, now, truth be told, I was a little bit nervous for her. Whereas I had spent ten months refining my submission, hers had been written at 3am, the morning that it was due in... following a lot of crying. But as I walked up to her I could see the relief on her face I knew that she too had passed. As I asked her how she had done, I kind of expected her to say that she had scraped by with a 40? 45? But no, with much joy and exuberance, she told me that she had got 63. 'Oh', I said. Well actually, the 'oh' was actually inside my head, what came out of my mouth was 'wow! That's amazing! I'm so pleased for you, I told you you could pull it off!' But inside my head, the 'oh' signified me going from being pleased and proud of my 58, to suddenly disappointed and ashamed of it, when it was compared to her 63. What minutes earlier had me celebrating the fact that I had passed my degree, suddenly felt inferior and shameful, when it was compared to somebody else.

Like Laura's story, the story of the prodigal son found in Luke 15 is an illustration of how comparison influences how we see the world around us and tarnishes even those moments that we have felt proud or content with our efforts and accomplishments. It robs those moments from us. In the story of the prodigal son, a family has been reunited after thinking they had lost their youngest child. The household were rejoicing at his return, but the older brother refused to join the welcoming committee.

This brother was the one who had stayed at home. He had worked hard for his family and had not let his father down. He hadn't run off to squander his inheritance like his younger sibling. He just faithfully got on with what he was meant to be doing. All was well until the younger brother returned. Now there was another person in the dance hall mirror and the older brother began to compare.

Suddenly the older brother became consumed with jealousy, grumbling, moaning and complaining about the way he had been treated until his father spoke up in Luke 15:9 'My son,' the father said, 'you are always with me, and everything I have is yours. But we had to celebrate and be glad, because this brother of yours was dead and is alive again; he was lost and is found. '

In other words, 'Stop looking at what your brother has and understand that you have everything you need right at your fingertips!'

You see, the older brother had his inheritance intact - despite the celebrations of the previous night, come morning, the younger brother would still be without his inheritance. Who knows, maybe he could work the fields to earn his living, but suffice to say the father is drawing the older brother's attention to the fact that he was looking in the mirror of comparison and seeing a distorted reflection.

The older brother's faithfulness meant that his inheritance was intact and he had access to all of his father's wealth. Yet all he could see in the dance hall studio mirror was that his brother had got away with so much compared to him, and his attitude became selfish, ungrateful and petty.

The older brother's comparison led to a relationship breakdown between him and his father, as well as a relationship breakdown between him and his brother. Comparison will rob us of our relationship with God if we become bitter about what we do or do not have compared to others. Comparison will rob us of our future when we disqualify ourselves because of what we feel we lack compared to others. Comparison will rob us of our peace when we allow others' lives to influence our view of our own. Its distorted reflection will make you think you are empty-handed when in fact you have full access to the Father, His blessing and your inheritance, right at your fingertips.

Protected by Gratitude

—

Gratitude is an antidote to comparison. One of the most effective ways to combat the thief of comparison is to cloak ourselves in gratitude.

When we choose gratitude over comparison we agree with the truth that everything good in our lives has come from God. His Word says that he gives us every good and perfect gift. Sometimes the difference between receiving or not receiving the gift is our attitude of thankfulness.

Luke 17 tells the story of ten lepers who asked Jesus to heal them. Only one of them returned to give thanks for the healing they had received and Jesus told him,

"Rise and go; your faith has made you well".

Luke 17:19 (NIV)

All of them received a good and perfect gift of healing, but only nine of them ever knew what it was like to be healed from leprosy. The one who had a thankful heart experienced the joy of being made whole.

When you look at what God did for that one leper compared to the other nine it may seem unfair. However, the same offer was open to all, but the outcome was determined by their attitudes, thoughts and responses to God. It is the same in our own lives.

A mirror can only ever reflect what we put in front of it, so the easy answer to avoiding the dance studio mirror is not to look in it. By refusing to enter into comparison and choosing to be thankful even in times of adversity and lack, we instantly shatter its power. **Our confidence is secure when it is built on the identity we see in God's Word, not on the one we have perceived in comparison to our peers.**

'Stop doing wrong, learn to do right.'

Isaiah 1:16

In the case of this particular mirror, I believe this is exactly what is needed. Stop looking in the mirror of comparison and learn to cloak yourself in thankfulness. I promise you this reflection will no longer have any power over you, in Jesus' Name.

Let's Get Practical
Be the Cheering Crowd

———

Mark Twain said that, "Comparison is the death of joy," and the science agrees. Research has found that comparison breeds feelings of envy, low-self confidence, and depression, as well as compromises our ability to trust others. Being in the cheering crowd is a decision that we each have to make - if you think about it, we are on the sidelines of everyone's life around us; the only race we are actually competing in is us, by ourselves! So we can either choose to be the sulky onlooker, wishing our trainers were like theirs, and our stride was that graceful, or we can be the cheering crowd! Making a decision that however nice their trainers, however much we admire what they are doing, we stay in our lane and remember our race is our own.

Here is a quick prayer that you can practically put into your routine when you feel the sulky onlooker start to emerge:

Dear Father,

I want to be a part of the cheering crowd for others, please help me to replace the spirit of comparison with the spirit of contentment and appreciation for others. I pray that you bless _____ that I have found I am comparing myself to.

In Jesus name,
Amen.

Not so social media

It takes on average 66 days to build a habit, and 22 days to break one, so time is on our side!! It's time to break some habits. In a world where the black hole of social media can steal away hours and hours of your valuable time, start putting into place some boundaries. Here are some tips to help you:

- Take some time to schedule in grabbing a cup of tea and sitting down to read His Word; this will help you to realign your truth with God's Truth.
- Ask Father God for a revelation that social media is not reality.
- Set a time you put your phone down at night.
- Make an intentional decision to make sure that social media is not the first thing you look at in the morning.
- Schedule in social media free days and see what you could do with your time instead of being online.
- Plan a 22 day schedule to break any unhealthy social media habits.

Prayer:

Lord, thank you for saving me. Thank you for taking disease, affliction, misery, pain, poverty, brokenness and every sin that this world is bound by on Your own shoulders.

Thank you that I now have access to all Your Kingdom has to offer. Thank you that when You look at me, You see only me and not my friends, my family or anyone else, just me. Lord, help me to do the same - to see myself in relation to You, not in comparison with others.

Father, I ask that You forgive my attitude of comparison and the jealousy and insecurity that has plagued me; and I ask that You would make my spirit sensitive to recognising when I slip back into these attitudes.

I commit to entering Your gates with thanksgiving and choose to shatter the mirror of comparison by remaining thankful at all times. Help me to do this by Your Spirit.

In Jesus' Name, Amen

Chapter 5
Tales of the Unexpected:
The Shop Window Reflection

It is the day of your all-important, dream job interview. You've spent ages choosing just the right outfit, hairstyle and make-up and you look great. You are feeling confident, the sun is shining and the train is running on time.

All of a sudden, it starts to rain and you realise you left your umbrella at home. The wind is blowing a gale and you also realise you also forgot to use waterproof mascara. With a sense of rising panic, it dawns on you that although the train isn't late, you are. You break into a run and trip up on the uneven pavement. With a sinking feeling you look down and see a broken heel dangling from your shoe and a large rip in your tights.

As you hobble past a shop window, you catch a glimpse of your reflection and it confirms all of your worst fears. Your 'up-do' is down, your mascara is giving you a 'gothic chick' look instead of the 'capable professional' look you were aiming for. With one heel on and one heel off, your confident 'I-have-it-all-together' look is as washed out as your hopes.

All that time and energy spent on getting ready, all of your optimism and hopes are dashed as this unexpected course of events. The shop window reflection confirms it, catches you off-guard and steals your opportunity. You turn around, watch the train leave without you and decide that the job clearly wasn't meant to be yours, so you might as well give up. It's the mirror of our circumstances, the unpredictability of life, and if we're looking in this one, then our sense of identity, value, strength and purpose will be determined by whether our life is going well or not.

It sounds like this:

'If my life is good, then God is good and so I feel good about myself. I'm a daughter of the King and He loves me. But if life is bad, then I'm a terrible person. This must be punishment and God doesn't love me anymore. He has forgotten me and maybe I'm not even saved!'

The thoughts, feelings and emotions that capture our attention when life throws us a curve-ball are what determine whether the outcome of those circumstances will destroy us or make us stronger.

The world we live in is unpredictable and has rough terrain called hurt, pain, fear, abuse, betrayal, disappointment, rebellion, mistrust and injustice to name but a few. And, whilst we don't have to like it, we do need to respond to it and not fear the sudden curve-balls of the unexpected shop window.

When Jesus commissioned us to go out into all the world and preach the good news, He knew the world would not give us a nice smooth, tarmac road but that life in this world would present us with; mud, rocks, hills and valleys. In 1 Thessalonians 3:3 (MSG) Paul writes:

1 Thessalonians 3:3 (MSG)

'Not that the troubles should come as any surprise to you. You've always known that we're in for this kind of thing. It's part of our calling. When we were with you, we made it quite clear that there was trouble ahead.'

1 Thessalonians 3:3 (MSG)

The 'trouble ahead' is not because God is punishing us. The trouble ahead is part of our living environment, our earth, which is still struggling under the weight of sin and corruption.

Trouble comes from us being on the receiving end of other people's bad choices, it can come from our own ignorance and disobedience, it can come through no fault of our own - sent by an enemy who comes to, 'kill, steal and destroy' us.

John 10:10 (NIV)

The thief comes only to steal and kill and destroy; I have come that they may have life, and have it to the full.

John 10:10 (NIV)

We cannot have a belief system built on the misconception that our status of 'Christian' is an automatic exemption from unexpected adversity and trials. In fact, the reality is that James 1 (NIV) indicates we would 'face trials of many kinds' - no exemptions are implied! What those trials develop in us though, depends entirely on how we respond to them and how we view God's part in it all.

Nor should we interpret our times of trial and adversity being a reflection of our good or bad behaviour or of God's character. We can be the innocent victims of other people's bad choices or we can be experiencing the consequences of our own poor decisions. Sometimes the trouble we face comes from hurt people hurting people and from living in a world that does not know God. Trouble comes from an enemy who kills, steals and destroys in every way he can. In Paul the apostle writes:

---

2 Corinthians 11:23-28 (MSG)

'I've worked much harder, been jailed more often, beaten up more times than I can count, and at death's door time after time. I've been flogged five times with the Jews' thirty-nine lashes, beaten by Roman rods three times, pummelled with rocks once. I've been shipwrecked three times, and immersed in the open sea for a night and a day. In hard journeys travelling year in and year out, I've had to ford rivers, fend off robbers, struggle with friends,

struggle with foes. I've been at risk in the city, at risk in the country, endangered by desert sun and sea storm, and betrayed by those I thought were my brothers. I've known drudgery and hard labour, many a long and lonely night without sleep, many a missed meal, blasted by the cold, naked to the weather. And that's not the half of it.'

2 Corinthians 11:23-28 (MSG) ────────────────────────────

Paul laid his life down for the faith; he was a good person, a godly person and yet bad things happened to him and around him. The fact is that bad things can and do happen to good people. The landscape of Paul's life was full of the hills and valleys of adversity and challenge and there were many times he was presented with the 'shop window reflection' of challenging circumstances where things were not going as planned. **The good news is that God never intended us to face the hills and valleys of our lives alone. He never intended for us to face a storm without a way to silence it.** Paul understood this and went on to write about God's response to his troubles in

──────────────────────────── 2 Corinthians 12:9 (MSG)

'My grace is enough; it's all you need. My strength comes into its own in your weakness.'

2 Corinthians 12:9 (MSG) ────────────────────────────

Paul goes on to write in verse 10:

──────────────────────────── 2 Corinthians 12:10 (MSG)

'Once I heard that, I was glad to let it happen. I quit focusing on the handicap and began appreciating the gift. It was a case of Christ's strength moving in on my weakness. Now I take limitations in stride, and with good cheer, these limitations that cut me down to size - abuse, accidents, opposition, bad breaks. I just let Christ take over! And so the weaker I get, the stronger I become.'

2 Corinthians 12:10 (MSG) ────────────────────────────

We need to understand that we do not have what it takes to navigate rough terrain in our own strength. But we can do it when we let Christ take over.

I faced one of these testing times in 2008 as I listened in shock as my Doctor told me that the lump they had just done a biopsy on would be sent away for tests. I had to wait a week for the results and there was about a 50 percent chance that I had cancer. During this unexpected situation, I had one of those God dreams that you never forget. In my dream I was reading

Psalm 23:5 (NIV)

"You prepare a table before me in the presence of my enemies".

Psalm 23:5 (NIV)

I saw myself dining at a huge round table with Wisdom on my right and Strength on my left. Around the table were seated Love, Hope, Faith, Joy and Peace. They were all interacting with me and chatting, as part of my circle of companions.

Then I became aware that over in the corner of the room were three shadowy figures called Fear, Worry and Unbelief and I asked God why they were there.

God replied saying, 'Life on earth is a public place, much like a restaurant, this is why the table is prepared in the presence of your enemies; Fear, Unbelief and Worry will always linger on the fringes of life, BUT who sits at YOUR table is by invitation only. Be very careful who you choose to keep company with.'

I could see that each time I looked over to where the three figures were huddled, they would look up to see if I was inviting them over. They inched closer and closer, peeking in over the goings on at my table, trying to see if I was giving them permission to take a seat.

Then, as I looked around the table, I saw that there were only enough seats for the companions I already had. God said, 'Your friends cannot stay if you give their seat to one of the three.' At that moment I saw Fear standing behind Faith, looking to see if I would give the nod and ask Faith to give up her seat.

This dream showed me that the battle I faced would be won or lost in my mind. Faith is a powerful weapon, and the first thing the enemy will try to do is separate you from the companions God has given to you to do your thought-life with.

During the wait for my test results, I learned what it means to take every thought captive and make it obedient to Christ. A process was taking place inside of me as I chose not to let the unexpected reflection of the 'shop window' stop me in my tracks and throw me off course.

I didn't have cancer, thank God, but I still won a battle. I won the battle for my peace of mind as I triumphed over Fear, and Faith stayed at my table.

Defeating Fear

—

Our deepest convictions about God are revealed during times of trial and adversity when life can feel very uncertain. Corrie ten Boom once said, "Never be afraid to trust an unknown future to a known God."

Yet so many of us fear the future. We fear what may or may not happen. When life is going well, we worry that the bubble will burst and when life is bad, we blame ourselves, God, those around us, or the church. By doing this we hand the enemy our peace.

I really struggled with this kind of fear after my first child was born. I loved him so much that I was frightened that something bad might happen to him and became obsessed with his safety.

Nights of sleeplessness were caused not just by needing to feed him but also by my fear. Was he breathing? Was he too hot or too cold,? Should he lie on his back, his front or his side?

You see, not long before my child was born, a couple close to us had lost their son to a still-birth at 29 weeks. They were the perfect Christian couple, leaders in the church and kind, good-hearted servants of God. Yet they lost their baby. As far as I could see, there was no safety, no assurance for me. If it could happen to them I thought it could happen to me, and suddenly I was caught by that shop window reflection.

God's answer to questions about our future health, wealth and security will always be the same. If you ask Him, like I did, He will probably just hold His hand out to you, smile affectionately and whisper, 'Do you trust Me?'

When we don't trust Him, we feed fear. When we question God's character and His intentions towards us, we allow unbelief and worry to dine with us.

There was a story I read amidst my battle with fear for my son's well-being, which helped me understand what God was after. It was about a couple whose baby daughter had been rushed to hospital with meningitis. They prayed and prayed and thankfully, in the morning, she had made it through the night and was going to recover. As the man and his wife were praising and thanking God for healing their precious baby and protecting her, they felt God say, 'Would you still praise me if she had died?'

If we really know God, know that He is good all the time, know that all things work together for the good of those who love Him and are called according to his purpose, then we do not have to fear an unknown future. It will not necessarily be without pain or heartache, but should difficult circumstances come we will not have to face them alone.

The Bible also says that we are more than conquerors. Do you know the difference between a conqueror and being more than a conqueror? **A conqueror wins a battle, but someone who is more than a conqueror wins the war.**

We are fighting a war for our peace, our trust in God, our intimacy and our relationship with Him. Life's circumstances can conspire against us to keep us far from Him, distrusting His intentions and fearing the future. We must choose to start speaking out the truth of God's Word, and choose to get to know Him more, even through life's challenges.

Choosing Joy in the Trial

———

I clearly recollect another time when this unexpected shop window reflection caught me head-on. An unexpected situation occurred which had the potential to devastate everything I had worked so hard for. That day as I caught my reflection in the shop window of my life, I could see my hopes and dreams fading fast.

I recall standing in my kitchen buttering bread. As I stood there, waves of despair crashed over me with such ferocity that I literally felt like I was drowning emotionally.

During this emotional onslaught **I heard the whisper of the Holy Spirit, quiet but intense. He said, 'Right now, at this very moment - choose joy.'**

It was probably one of the most ridiculous things God had ever said to me. Joy was the furthest thing from my mind and the emotions I was experiencing were so opposed to joy, I had no idea how to choose it.

But as I stood there, an old Sunday school song came to mind. It goes something like this;

'Rejoice in the Lord always, again I say rejoice.
Rejoice in the Lord always, again I say rejoice.
Rejoice, rejoice, again I say rejoice.
Rejoice, rejoice, again I say rejoice. '

I started to hum it softly, then to whisper it until within a few minutes I was pacing up and down my kitchen, waving a bread knife in my hand singing the command over myself.

As I sang and refused to let the negative emotions drown out my voice, I could feel joy begin to bubble up inside and with it came strength. This was not a joy that I had generated because I had no reason to be joyful. The joy that bubbled up came straight from God. All I did was choose to make room for it. As it says in Nehemiah 8:10 (NIV) 'The joy of the Lord is your strength. '

Within minutes of this happening another scripture came to mind which was:

James 1:2-4 (NLT)

"Dear brothers and sisters, when troubles of any kind come your way, consider it an opportunity for great joy. For you know that when your faith is tested, your endurance has a chance to grow. So let it grow, for when your endurance is fully developed, you will be perfect and complete, needing nothing."

James 1:2-4 (NLT)

God's Mirror Will Make You Laugh at the Days to Come

Proverbs 31 shows us a mirror image of a woman of God, it says :

Proverbs 31:25-26 (NIV)

'She is clothed with strength and dignity, she can laugh at the days to come.'

Proverbs 31:25-26 (NIV)

So, the Proverbs 31 woman is laughing at the days to come, even though she has no idea whether those days contain good circumstances or bad circumstances. She knows that bad news may come but she has no fear of it.

When we choose to look into God's mirror, our laughter is not dependant on our circumstances. Our laughter will come from the knowledge of God in our lives, from the sense of security and comfort that He brings. He is your Rock, your Deliverer, your Tower of Strength and when you look in His mirror, you may not be able to see all of your future but you can be confident that whether there be good times or bad times ahead, God is God and He is good.

When you learn that, you know that you will be able to laugh at the days to come, because when you look in his mirror, you will see not just who you are but who he is and if you choose to believe it, no circumstance will ever take you away from your sense of identity and security.

Paul the apostle knew this, as it says in

Philippians 4:11-13 (NIV)

"I have learned to be content whatever the circumstances. I know what it is to be in need, and I know what it is to have plenty. I have learned the secret of being content in any and every situation, whether well fed or hungry, whether living in plenty or in want. I can do everything through him who gives me strength."

Philippians 4:11-13 (NIV)

Philippians 4:7 (AMPC) also tells us that if we learn to rejoice in the Lord always, whether the circumstances we face are good or bad, we are promised a certain type of peace. It says:

Philippians 4:7 (AMPC)

"And God's peace shall be yours, that tranquil state of a soul assured of its salvation through Christ, and so fearing nothing from God and being content with its earthly lot of whatever sort that is, that peace] which transcends all understanding shall garrison and mount guard over your hearts and minds in Christ Jesus."

Philippians 4:7 (AMPC)

God's peace is the only kind of peace that will get you through life in an unpredictable world that does not guarantee you a pain-free journey.

In other words, God's peace surpasses the reflection of the 'Shop Window' that would have you believe you are a lost cause. His peace is not dependent on what your reflection looks like or what your circumstances are. His peace protects you as you look at those circumstances and decide to praise Him anyway.

I believe the early church found that kind of peace when they sang His praise as they were being fed to the lions. I believe Esther found that peace when she said, "If I perish, I perish." (Esther 4:16, NIV) I believe James found that peace when he told us to, "Consider it pure joy, my brothers and sisters, whenever you face trials of many kinds." (James 1:2, NIV) I believe Mary found that kind of peace when she said, "May everything you have said about me come true" (Luke 1:38, NLT).

I believe that when she had lost everything, Ruth had that peace when she said to Naomi, "Where you go I will go, and where you stay I will stay. Your people will be my people and your God my God." (Ruth 1:16, NIV) And I believe Jesus had that peace when he said "not my will but yours be done" (Luke 22:42, NIV).

We can have that peace when we refuse to let our lives be shaken by circumstances and instead say, 'I trust you Lord, you are good to me, I know I am not alone in this trial and I choose to rejoice. '

When the unexpected happens, when crisis hits your life, that's when the mirror of His Word will show you not just your reflection, but His too. Whatever the unexpected circumstance you are facing, when you catch your disheveled, panicked reflection in the shop window, just know that you'll see Jesus standing right next to you too, if you look close enough. As you gaze at Him, as you draw close to Him, it will be His peace that guards your heart and your mind.

Mercy UK's Chief Operating Officer and my sister, Debbie Harvie, started her Mercy journey as a resident in the US home where she learnt what it means to deal with the 'Shop Window Reflection'. This is her story:

"Born and raised in a Christian home, I was taught that God was my protector, my provider, my Father. I grew up listening to and learning about God. I knew the Bible stories and I believed that God was everything the Bible said about Him.

"But when I was 12 years old, it seemed that all I had been taught was a lie. I was manipulated into a full sexual relationship with a drug dealer 10 years my senior. He introduced me to the 'benefits' of getting high on drugs and gradually he groomed and seduced me into a sexually abusive relationship with him.

"Suddenly, the normal Christian life I had been brought up in, changed dramatically. Every day for three years was the same, hidden with the same lie that all was fine, but it wasn't. I got into fights, began cutting myself and even tried to commit suicide, but it didn't work. I felt like I couldn't tell anyone because I thought it was all my fault.

"I was caught in a spiral of helplessness and shame, and my anger burned against a God who should have protected me, who could have stopped it or told someone about the abuse I was suffering. I renounced God and vowed to live my life outside of Him.

"I had no hope, no future, no peace, no truth; just pain, despair, shame and the lies of the enemy tormenting my mind constantly. The root causes of my pain were not being dealt with and I desperately needed help.

"I remembered a book my sister gave me about Mercy, and as I read it, I knew there was hope; I knew there was a place that could help me.

"At Mercy, I learnt that we all have personal choices, and that sadly some of us become the victims of other people's bad choices. God did not send the abuse because the Bible teaches that every good and perfect gift comes from God and abuse is neither of those things. The enemy comes to steal, kill and destroy, and so abuse in all its forms has its roots well and truly in his territory.

"I now know that God has provided freedom from the abuse through the power of the cross and redemption. I have learnt to forgive, and in doing so, have found that the hurt, pain and destruction I was facing have been processed and dealt with, with God at my side.

"Now, over 18 years after I graduated from Mercy, I am happily married, serving in my local church, raising two children after nearly three years of trying to conceive and I have the privilege of serving as part of the leadership of Mercy UK. Only God can bring about that kind of transformation!"

Let's get Practical
Stop the cycle

____

As I said earlier, it is so important to take every thought captive (2 Corinthians 10:5), cycles of bad thoughts can instigate anything from anxious feelings to longer term depressive states. We think about what they said to us, what they might be thinking about us, what you said that you shouldn't, how you want the situation to be different. This is a state of looking in our shop window mirror until we can't see anything other than our disappointment. But here are 3 strategies to help you to be present and focus on the here and now, and the direction of moving forward.

1. Grounding yourself

Now, this sounds really simple, but it really does work. It can help you switch your focus from the rear-view mirror, back to the windshield. Grounding yourself is all about making use of your senses. Taste, touch, smell, sound and sight.

So when you are feeling overwhelmed with the rearview mirror reflection, look around you, what can you see?

Take your shoes off and feel the ground beneath your feet. You can use oils to ignite your smell sense and that can help to ground yourself, but these are just ideas! You can do it anyway you like, as long as you are using your senses!

2. Gratitude List

What are you grateful for? This is often something we were told by the older generations 'be grateful for what you have...' but this old saying has in fact received scientific backing! It has been proven that gratitude is the only emotion that you can feel completely on its own.

So if you are in a cycle of unhappiness, anger, jealousy - thinking in a grateful mindset can literally stop the cycle. Once again, go back to who you want to invite to your table!

So grab a pen and get writing, the gratitude list can be from the smallest things to the biggest things and watch your mindset change!

3. Tell a better narrative

In your life, God is the master author - but YOU are the narrator. You get to decide how what perspective you take on your story. You get to decide the tone of what happens, and sometimes what we say and our narration, is very different...

[Friend: What do you think?
Me: Oh well, it's not the end of the world!
Narrator: It was, in fact, the end of the world.....]

The narrator in our head can steer us in different directions, it can interpret situations as positive or negative, as the end of the world or a bump in the road. It is important that we listen to the narrative we are giving ourselves and see if it matches up to what God says about us, our lives and our reflection. And if you catch yourself with a negative narrative, a harsh narrative, a talking-yourself-down narrative, take a minute to change the narrative to what God is speaking over you and speak it over yourself.

Prayer:

Lord, thank you that Your love surpasses human love. That Your love is not dependent upon whether or not I feel worthy of it; that it is constant, without beginning or end no matter what circumstances I face.

Thank you for the promise that You WILL make ALL things work for good for those who love You. Help me to see You at work in every situation, in the calm and in the storms.

Help me to not hide away from the adversities that come my way but to walk through them holding Your hand, secure in the knowledge that Your strength is made perfect in my weakness, that You are growing me through situations that the enemy meant for harm and are leading me to a higher level of faith, trust and joy.

Father, show me the patterns of thought in my mind that are not of You. I want to get rid of everything that hinders me from grabbing hold of my present and my future. Show me what You say about me. I choose today to feed faith and starve fear.

I choose to look adversity in the face and I choose to declare joy over my circumstances. I laugh at the days to come and declare You are greater than my troubles, because the bigger I see You, the smaller they become. Thank you for Your Truth that sets me free.

In Jesus' name, Amen.

IT'S
OKAY
IF IT
TAKES
TIME
YOU
DIDN'T
GET TO
WHERE
YOU
ARE
NOW
OVERNIGHT

Aimee Wood @bloommydear_

Chapter 6
Know, Believe, Do:
The Compact Mirror

———

There is one type of mirror which every girl should carry. It can be taken with her wherever she goes and can be used whenever she needs it. It's there in emergencies, for the odd touch up and is one of the essentials to be found in every woman's handbag. It's a compact mirror and this is the kind of mirror God's Word is to our lives; always there inside our hearts in case of emergencies, or simply because we want to check something - easy to get to, often used.

Just like you can't see your reflection in a mirror unless you look into it, you can't see your true reflection unless you look in the true mirror that is His Word.

Let's remind ourselves of what it says about God's compact mirror in:

James 1:22-25 (NIV)

"Do not merely listen to the word, and so deceive yourselves. Do what it says. Anyone who listens to the word but does not do what it says is like someone who looks at his face in a mirror and, after looking at himself, goes away and immediately forgets what he looks like. But whoever looks intently into the perfect law that gives freedom, and continues in it—not forgetting what they have heard, but doing it—they will be blessed in what they do."

James 1:22-25 (NIV)

It couldn't be clearer; if we want to know what we really look like there is only one mirror that can reflect our true image that is not distorted by our past or our insecurities.

There is only one mirror that does not compare us with others or change what it shows us, depending on our circumstances. It is the mirror of God's Word. Its reflection is constant, unchanging and it shows us who we really are.

Know, Believe, Do.

___

As every girl knows, it is possible to gaze at your reflection in the mirror for a very long time. But simply looking will never change anything about us. When we look in the mirror of God's Word, if we want it to impact our lives we must respond to what we see and then do something about it.

Let's remind ourselves,

James 1:25 (NIV)

"...But whoever looks intently into the perfect law that gives freedom, and continues in it—not forgetting what they have heard, but doing it..."

James 1:25 (NIV)

Not only should our look into God's mirror be done intently, (that means closely, purposefully, keenly, with intent), we must continue to stay in God's Word. Not just a one-off read every now and again, but a sustained lifestyle of reading and learning what the Word of God says about us. If you want to find your identity, your worth and your true value as laid out in the Word, then you need to put the effort in and read it, because that's how you'll begin to know.

Knowing God's Word is crucial, because unless we know what it says how can we ever know what to believe?

Sadly, we are not born with a scholarly knowledge of the Word of God already embedded in our hearts. We are required to learn it, to read it and to listen to it. Everyone learns in different ways, so try and find out the best way for you.

Soak It Up

———

Just touching the Word is not enough; absorbing it is what matters. If I were to spill a glass of water, I could choose to mop it up with a sponge or with a newspaper. Mopping it up with a newspaper would mean that the paper would get wet, but very little would be absorbed and most would just roll off the page, back onto the floor. However, if I used a sponge, it would completely absorb the water. That's how we need to be with the Word of God.

Many people put much effort into knowing the Word but then they neglect to listen for His Voice. In John 10:27 (KJV), Jesus said, "My sheep hear My voice...".

The Bible is God's love letter to the world and the more you soak up, the more you will grow to love it and recognise His voice through it.

Without God's Word, it is difficult to learn to recognise His Voice, but without knowing His Voice, the Bible is just a book. It is through a relationship with the Holy Spirit that the Bible is revealed as more than the ancient words of an unseen God. It becomes a clear and consistent message of God's love for His people and for living life His way in freedom and relationship with Him.

Knowing how you learn means you can become absorbent, like a sponge. We come across the term 'hearing God's Voice' so often in church circles that we forget that it isn't always about 'hearing' His Voice, but about learning to recognise it. Some of us absorb new information by reading and writing, others learn by doing, whilst others prefer to listen to someone else explain it to us. These same learning styles reflect the different ways we might recognise the voice of God in our lives.

Over the page are examples of different learning styles.
Take a minute to look at which type you identify with the most.

You learn best through seeing and visualising.

VISUAL LEARNER

You learn best through doing and moving.

KINESTHETIC LEARNER

You learn best through listening and speaking.

AUDITORY LEARNER

You learn best through reading and writing

READ/WRITE LEARNER

To help you absorb the Word of God, have a go at using strategies from which learning style you most relate with (be aware that most people are a combination of a few of these styles), for example:

If you are mostly an auditory learner you could try downloading an audible version and listen to the Word being read. There are hundreds of Bible apps available that will help you find creative ways of saturating your life with God's Truth. Additionally, reading it out loud can particularly be helpful as there is something very powerful about speaking the truth of God's Word over yourself.

If you are a visual learner you could put colourful sticky notes of key scriptures around your car, your bedroom, or on your fridge door or try creating amazing imagery in your mind and bring scripture to life through your imagination. Also, you could draw pictures about what God may be showing you through different scriptures, to really visualise His Word.

If you are a read/write learner you could take notes about each scripture and look up commentaries of the Bible, from a study bible or online. There is also a range of Bible apps which include commentaries. If you are mostly a read/write learner you will probably thrive from just reading the Word yourself!

If you are an action learner you could try setting challenges for yourself based on your studies of the Bible such as those set in our Reflections cards. Sometimes pacing or putting dance to the scriptures you are memorising or meditating on will help. And, if you are creative as well, you might want to focus some of your art or creative writing or music on what the Truth of God's Word means to you. Combine these strategies to suit how you learn and you will find that the Word of God will become really familiar to you and enable you to recognise His Voice as it will always be in line with His Word.

Changing The Software

—

You can read the Word, listen to it, go to theological college, write books about it, even do all the strategies I've mentioned - but if you don't believe what the Word says, then you will never see the true reflection it can show you.

James 1:6 (NIV)

'You must believe and not doubt, because he who doubts is like a wave of the sea, blown and tossed by the wind...you will be unstable in all you do.'

James 1:6 (NIV)

As we are reading, hearing and speaking the Word, there is a key aspect that must be in play if we are ever going to be free from the old, distorted reflections; we must choose to believe it.

Believing what the Word says is fundamental to everything written in this book. If you don't believe it, then you will continue to be deceived by the reflections of the other false mirrors offering you a distorted reflection of your identity. You'll become confused, sure of who you are one minute and doubting the next. Your life will become unstable, and your confidence, sense of worth and value, will be tossed to and fro by the waves of opinion, circumstances, or by your own internal belief system that simply says, "No, this cannot be true".

Our internal belief system is shaped by our childhood, environment, socio-economic background, and by experiences, circumstances and consequences of choices outside of our control. For many of us this internal wiring is faulty and sets us up for failure. Our belief system leads us to believe the false reflections of the mirrors described in this book.

Believing is a choice and it's a choice only you can make. Your vicar, pastor, friend, parent, youth leader or family can talk about how much God loves you and what the Bible says about your identity. But if there's something in you that doesn't accept or believe the Truth, you will filter their words without taking in the Truth contained in them and your internal belief system will remain unchanged.

Unless you make a conscious decision to believe what God says through His Word, unless you choose to believe the mirror image He shows you, you will be trapped in a world of unbelief and nothing will change.

Mercy UK graduate Jordan-Louise said;

"Over my 6 months at Mercy I began a transformation which has been ultimately life changing. We were in study one evening when I came across Psalm 139:13-14 "For you created my inmost being; you knit me together in my mother's womb. I praise you because I am fearfully and wonderfully made." This spoke to my soul. I had always been under the impression that I was a mistake, but God doesn't make mistakes! He sewed me together with love, with precision and for a purpose. Over the coming months I started learning to listen to His Word more and take notice. My flaws started to become my strengths, because I am unique, I AM fearfully and wonderfully made. Don't get me wrong, every day is a battle to walk in the Truths I am learning, but I know that with God by my side I am equipped to deal with my battles in a healthier way. I continue to fight and walk tall."

Jordan-Louise's sense of identity, worth and value came into line with what God said about her when she chose to believe Him and live her life based on His Truth.

Faith to Step Out

In the old 1989 movie 'Indiana Jones and the Last Crusade', Indiana is involved in a search for the Holy Grail, the cup from which Christ drank at the Last Supper. As the film reaches its climax, Indy must go through three tests in order to reach it.

After overcoming the first two obstacles, the final test requires Indy to step out in faith. He stands at the edge of a wide chasm with no visible way across the divide and yet the book his father gave him tells him to step out and believe.

His adversary says, "It's time to ask yourself what you believe." And as Indy stands facing the vast chasm before him, he has a choice to make. Will he follow the instructions from his father's book and place his faith in what it instructs him to do, or will he base his belief on what he can see with his natural eyes?

In the next room, his father whispers over and over, "You must believe boy, you must believe..."

As Indy takes a deep breath and makes a choice within himself to trust his father, he steps into the void. And to his amazement, his foot comes down on solid ground! A bridge appears across the chasm that had been there all along but was hidden from Indy's view.

Every time we look in the mirror of God's Word and are presented with a true reflection of who we are, we have a choice to make. Believe what it says and act accordingly, or walk away and forget it.

The choice is not a difficult one but so often we complicate it with thoughts and feelings and fears. In the end, it is all about choosing who and what we believe.

"This commandment that I'm commanding you today isn't too much for you, it's not out of your reach. It's not on a high mountain - you don't have to get mountaineers to climb the peak and bring it down to your level and explain it before you can live it. And it's not across the ocean - you don't have to send sailors out to get it, bring it back, and then explain it before you can live it. No. The word is right here and now - as near as the tongue in your mouth, as near as the heart in your chest. Just do it!"

Deuteronomy 30:11-14 (MSG)

The commandment God gave the Israelites was to choose life, to live believing His Word and to act according to it. It is still the same for us today. Will you believe the mirror of His Word? Will you choose to continue looking in it and apply what you read to your everyday life? If you do, you will begin to see the true reflection of who you are. Your confidence will become firmly rooted in Him and the foundations of your life become strong.

There is immense power and freedom in choosing to believe God's Word about our identity. I believe it's one of the reasons there is such an attack on the self-esteem, confidence and sense of worth of so many women. As one of our graduates shared,

"God is showing me that He doesn't want me to be the image that I think I need to be but the image He wants me to be."

The enemy knows that if we believe our true reflection in God's mirror, we will become an unstoppable force to be reckoned with and our world will change.

Let's Get Practical
Find your Truth

––––

This tip is to help you build your God-esteem. You need to pick your truth, so when the lies flood in, or you're relying on others to build your self esteem, you have something to fall back on and remind yourself of. Remember, that the Word of God is your greatest weapon in the battle against false reflections.

–– *Hebrews 4:12 (NIV)*

"For the Word of God is alive and active. Sharper than any double-edged sword, it penetrates even to dividing soul and spirit, joints and marrow; it judges the thoughts and attitudes of the heart."

Hebrews 4:12 (NIV) ––

FALSE REFLECTION

I am unlovable and unworthy. If you knew the real me, you would reject me. No one really likes me.

GOD'S TRUTH

With God's help, I will learn to be myself and trust him to bring people into my life that will appreciate me and respect me for who I am. My worth is in who God says I am.

"But the very hairs on your head are numbered. Do not fear therefore; you are of more value than many sparrows."

Luke 12:7

FALSE REFLECTION

Even when I do my best, it is not good enough. I can never meet the standard.

GOD'S TRUTH

I am fully loved, completely accepted, and totally pleasing to God. Regardless of how much I do or fail to do, I will remain fully loved, completely accepted, and totally pleasing to God.

"If the Lord delights in a man's way, he makes his steps firm; although he stumble, he will not fall, for the Lord upholds him with his hand."

Psalm 37:23-24.

FALSE REFLECTION

I will always be insecure and fearful. I am a bad person.

GOD'S TRUTH

I can be confident in him who created me. I will draw my security, courage, and identity from what God says about me.

"For God did not give us a spirit of timidity, but a spirit of power, of love and of self-discipline."

2 Timothy 1:7

FALSE REFLECTION

I always make wrong decisions. I am unable to take care of myself or make wise decisions. I am out there all alone.

GOD'S TRUTH

I choose to believe that God will help me to make wise decisions as I ask him for direction for my life. If I align my decisions with the word of God, I will consistently make the right choice. God will protect me and keep me.

"If any of you lacks wisdom, he should ask God, who gives generously to all without finding fault, and it will be given to him."

James 1:5

Prayer:

God, thank you that You have made it easy for us to access You. Thank you that we have the freedom to open our Bibles or pray at any time throughout the day.

Help me to make opening the 'compact mirror' of Your Word a regular practice. Let Your living Word change my thoughts and actions.

I ask You to make every part of me whole. Give me a passion and thirst for absorbing Your Word. Holy Spirit, help me to hear Your Voice in everything I do, that I would choose to walk in line with the Truth.

As I read the Bible and walk with You, I commit to work in partnership with You to break down any faulty internal belief systems from my past and create new software.

Today, I choose to believe that in You, I am a force to be reckoned with and that I am changing the course of my future and of the people attached to my life for Your glory.

In Jesus' name, Amen.

Chapter 7
Becoming the Mirror

———

There once was a group of women doing a Bible study on the book of Malachi. As they were studying chapter three they came across verse three (NIV) which says:

Malachi 3:3

"He will sit as a refiner and purifier of silver."

Malachi 3:3

This verse puzzled the women and they wondered what this meant. One of the women offered to find out about the process of refining silver and report back to the group. She was so intrigued by the verse that she made an appointment to watch a silversmith at work. She didn't mention anything to him about the reason for her interest beyond her curiosity about the process of refining silver. As she watched the silversmith, he held a piece of silver over the fire and let it heat up. He explained that when refining silver, you have to hold the silver in the middle of the fire where the flames were hottest to burn away all the impurities.

She asked the silversmith if it was true that he had to sit in front of the fire while the silver was being refined. The man answered that yes, he had to sit there holding the silver and he had to keep his eyes on the silver the entire time it was in the fire. For if the silver was left for just a moment too long in the flames, it would be destroyed. The woman was silent for a moment. Then she asked, 'How do you know when the silver is fully refined? 'He smiled at her and answered, Oh, that's the easy part - it's when I see my image reflected in it.'

When we stop looking in false mirrors; when we start believing the reflection God's mirror shows us, we will begin to reflect His glory. Our lives become a mirror that shows others who He is.

2 Corinthians 3:18 (NIV)

"And we, who with unveiled faces all reflect the Lord's glory, are being transformed into his likeness with ever increasing glory, which comes from the Lord."

2 Corinthians 3:18 (NIV)

The great work that God does inside of us is about more than us living a good Christian life and becoming nice, well-balanced people. It's not just about us. There is a world out there full of brokenness, pain and people who do not know their creator. **Ultimately, when we break away from the distorted mirror reflections** described in this book and learn to look into the mirror of His Word, **we become a people who are able to reflect all He is to those around us.**

Extraordinarily Ordinary

Over the years, I've seen how some people have gone through terrible traumas yet still proclaimed God's Truth. God has responded by using their lives to touch others in a powerful way. They have allowed God to turn the furnace sent to destroy them into a beacon of hope, and their stories inspire thousands to overcome all obstacles and rise above the hardship to bring glory to God.

Yet I have also seen how God has used those who have no great story of dramatic rescue but who have discovered their identity, worth and value in Him amidst the quietness of an ordinary looking life.

God will use the broken, the lonely, the abused, the disenfranchised or the whole, the happy and the content. He uses whoever makes themselves available to Him. He changes each of us, moulds and shapes us, heals the hurts and in His Hands we become more than we could ever dream of.

Don't ever disqualify yourself for any reason - neither the shame of your past nor the favour of your past are reasons not to enter into the purpose God has placed on your life.

A mirror has no choice but to reflect what is in front of it. The mirror of His Word reflects anyone who chooses to place themselves in front of it, regardless of their circumstances or background.

It's one of the great joys of my life to watch as broken and distorted reflections find their complete mirror image in the face of our God as He transforms the lives of the young women at Mercy UK. What excites me even more is when those same young women, once so broken and trapped, go on to transform others in their communities through the power of their true reflection.

I don't know what heroes look like to you but the women whose stories you are about to read are some of mine...

Sarah's Story

"My body - I'm not sure at what point I began to hate it. As a child I don't remember thinking about it because, I guess, my biggest worries as a 7 year old as for the majority of us, was trying to prevent the person sitting next to me from copying my spelling test answers...

Perhaps it was never having anyone affirm me as beautiful - whatever that even meant. Or being teased and called names by my brothers - even in jest.

Perhaps it was when I went to school and was aggressively bullied for over a year and called all sorts of awful and degrading things.

Perhaps it was growing up with ginger hair and always being laughed at - even by grown men. "She'd be hot - if she wasn't ginger." Comments like that. They stung.

Perhaps it was the relationship I was in that taught me from far too young an age that my body was not my own, it was a piece of meat, something to be both desired and then spat out. Simultaneously.

Perhaps it was all these things. But my body became something that was both repulsive and to be feared. My boundaries felt violated, my 'no' never heard and I think that was partly why anorexia became so safe to me. It hid me. It made my body as repulsive as I already felt inside. It made it undesirable - untouchable. My teenage years, those crucial identity forming years had been filled with a lot of pain, a lot of lies, a lot of deceit, a lot of manipulation. And so I emerged as a confused, broken girl with no clue about who she was, or even what she looked like.

How people saw me, what people thought of me became everything to me. Wanting to be seen and loved and liked by my peers, that felt like the goal. It felt like that would affirm me as beautiful. If I could be popular. If I could have 'the guy' then somehow I would have attained that elusive thing we call 'beauty'. I thought that would make me happy. But it didn't. I had to live many different lives to be all those things to all those people. I had mask after mask on and with each layer I lost sight again and again of who I was. It's a horrible thing, to finally reach that goal that you've been aiming for and then realise that you're more miserable and broken than you were when you started, and that you've had to sacrifice so much of yourself to get there.

When I looked in the mirror, all I saw was failure. And fear. And disgust. And unworthiness. And humiliation. And degradation. And insignificance. My goal to be liked became channeled into fixating on a number on a scale. I was in love with the bones I could feel on my body - but when I looked in the mirror I couldn't see them. I didn't see myself as 'fat' - I didn't see a giant blob that I think some people expect of people with body dysmorphia. Mine was more subtle than that. I could see I wasn't obese but I couldn't see what I really looked like. As I endlessly felt my arms, my legs, my back I would feel a rush of satisfaction at the sharpness my hands were met with. But when I looked in the mirror it wasn't enough. My body was never good enough just as I believed I was never good enough.

When I went to Mercy 10 years ago everything changed. I met Jesus. And for the first time I began to hear His voice and what He had to say about me. I began to immerse myself in His Word and wash myself in the Truth that I am fearfully and wonderfully made, a masterpiece of design, hand-crafted, hand-made. I saw that He had come so close; that the God of all creation who holds the universe in His hands had come so close to knit me together. In my quiet times with Him He would whisper to me 'there is no flaw in you'.

I began to experience His delight of me, in me, and I began to live from that place. And that is where I have remained. 10 years on I still choose to live from what He says about me. My need for others' approval or compliment has diminished. I know who I am because He tells me. I feel free. I feel like I can breathe again. I no longer detest my body and I no longer punish it.

I used to say that you could line up the entire population of the world and have them all tell me that I am beautiful and I still wouldn't have believed them. It's ironic then, that I now live the life of a missionary with my husband and family in South Africa and from the overflow of what God has done in me, tell others that they are beautiful, brave and the beloved of Jesus.

My prayer is always, that my words of encouragement leads them to a place of truly recognising that He is Truth, because truly nothing compares to knowing the Father's voice and you've let His thoughts, His words and His opinions define you. Nothing can touch that."

Hannah's Story

"Being born with a cleft lip and palate, I was measured right up until the age of 18; every inch of my face was measured, poked, prodded, pulled this way, pushed that way, tucked here and tugged there. The more insecure I got, the more spurred on the surgeons were to 'fix' me. I believed the lie that because of my difference, I was not beautiful. Not because they had ever said that but because I was allowing my own self-worth to be based upon the outcome of the next surgery. It took 17 surgeries later for me finally to say... I'm done. Unfortunately, I had to reach rock bottom to get there.

My most terrifying experience was with the last surgery I had, which consisted of rhinoplasty (nose job!), implants being screwed into my cheeks and my whole cleft being cut open, just to be stitched back up into a straighter position. I remember, afterwards; the nurse telling me that I might want to wait a couple of days before looking in the mirror because some people can find it quite a shock. Being the person I was, I couldn't wait. So, at the first opportunity, with no-one else around; I walked into the bathroom and came face to face with myself in the mirror. It was then that I broke. I wailed and wailed asking myself 'what have I done?'. All I could see that was remotely familiar to me, was my eyes. The rest of my face was swollen, bruised, with blood filling up my nose and stitches running above my lip. I went home and silently fell into complete despair. I just couldn't adjust to the shock of 'my new face'. My family were and always have been, incredibly supportive but there wasn't anything that anyone could say to make me feel better.

In the following months, I ended up having a breakdown and it's only looking back that I realise that this surgery had played a big part in this.

The way I felt about my face had a big impact on my self-esteem. Make-up became my shield and I would avoid speaking to people if I didn't feel confident enough, or if I felt there was any risk of them judging me.

I was only a teenager when I applied to Mercy UK. I had very little confidence and overwhelming insecurities and I applied desperately hoping that I wouldn't be judged. My immediate thought was that there was no way that I'd ever be able to change the way I feel about myself. I really thought I was going to be stuck in this mindset forever. But I wanted something to change and I was willing to give it a try and God had His plans.

During my time at Mercy, I was not judged or measured by my looks. Instead, I was challenged to look into a new mirror, to no longer refer to the mirror on the wall, rather; the mirror of God's Word. The more and more I read His statements of what He thought of me and how He viewed me, the more I began to hear it. I mean really hear it, like believe it. My roots of unbelief were teased out and carefully replanted into God's love. I realised that I had spent my life basing my worth on my outside appearance, assuming that if I could have a more symmetrical face and just be a bit skinnier, then I could be happier. Wrongly, I thought that everyone else was judging me in the same way. But when I changed mirrors, I saw that I also had a heart and a soul and a personality. 1 Samuel 16 tells us that God sees things differently. That we judge by outward appearance, but the Lord looks at the heart. The more I realised that God actually liked me, the more I learnt to like myself.

It's been 12 years since I left Mercy and I live my life now knowing that I will never allow myself to become consumed by my 'imperfect' face again. Beauty begins on the inside and oh how good it is to know that in His eyes He sees no stain, no flaw... just beauty.

I now teach private vocal lessons which was a big step for me. I had to enter into a newer level of vulnerability to put myself out there and so I decided to just let God have control on this one and it's been so worth it to be able to see others grow in their own confident-vulnerability as they find their voice.

My prayer for you today is within Ephesians 3:17-18 'Then Christ will make his home in your heart as you trust Him. Your roots will grow down into God's love and keep you strong. And may you have the power to understand, as all God's people should, how wide, how long, how high and how deep His love is'. I hope you too will change your mirror and replace it with the Word of God. This is the only true reflection you will ever need to see."

Naomi's Story

"I have been married 3 years now and have a 1 year old son, he is amazing. I knew that pregnancy was going to change my body and I was worried about that but I underestimated how incredible my body actually is. My body grew this perfect human from 2 single cells and carried him safely for 9 months! Not only that but my body then produced milk to sustain him and grow him into the toddler he is now. There are days when I struggle with my postpartum body, I look at the stretch marks and the cesarean scar and don't like what I see but God's truths about me are bigger than my doubts. I have not "sprung back" to my pre-pregnancy body or weight that you see celebrities doing in the magazines and sometimes I feel like that means my husband won't love my body anymore but I couldn't be more wrong. He loves my body and is so proud or our son that it created. Sometimes, I will be lying in bed and my son will come over, lift up my top and kiss my stretch marks, almost as though he knows what they symbolise. He absolutely loves my tummy!

When I look back to 7 years ago when I was in the depths of anorexia I remember feeling like I would never love my body and that I would hate myself for getting over a certain weight. But I also remember the time my doctor sat me down and warned me that if I carried on losing weight for a long period of time then having children of my own would not be possible. Now I have a toddler and I am so thankful for God's faithfulness in my life. I still struggle sometimes to love my body but I'm on a journey and I know that as long as I'm on this journey holding God's hand then I'm on the winning team.

I look at my stretch marks and I am reminded about "Kintsugi", the Japanese art of mending broken pottery by filling in the cracks with gold, making the item more unique and valuable.

Something that was broken and could have been thrown out was given a second life and was made more unique and valuable in the process. I live knowing that I have been born again into a new life, that the old Naomi has gone and this new Naomi wears her golden scars proudly knowing what's been accomplished. While I was at Mercy I went through a transformation, almost like a caterpillar becoming a butterfly. And no matter how much I struggle with my body image I know butterflies can't stuff themselves back into their cocoons. I can never go back to the place I was before Mercy because I have been completely transformed, I am a different person.

I'm now working for a mental health charity and looking after my son, Elijah, who is now 16 months old. I'm also doing youth work at our church on a Friday for the young people who live in the area, most of whom have never been to church before. It' really exciting being the person they know as a Christian and breaking the stereotypes that they have built up.

I've had a passion to work with youth since my time at Mercy, simply because most of my problems started in teenagehood. For the sake of the young people, I am determined to be the person I needed when I was that age, and to reflect the truth that their self-worth and identity is not found in the world, but is found in the very heart of our Heavenly Father."

Esme's Story

"'My scars don't define me,' 'My scars are not who I am,' 'There is no shame,' - These are some of the common phrases that would come out of my mouth for many years. But the reality is, that is not how I felt on the inside. The stares on the bus, the whispers behind your back, hearing the passer by say it's disgusting, the mum shushing as a young child asks what's on that girl's arms... All of those things added to my internal shame, yet the words that came out of my mouth remained the same. The truth is though, as much as I said it, I just didn't believe it and I certainly didn't feel it. At a time where God was even physically healing the scars of others and I was hearing the testimonies of scars disappearing before their eyes, I began to resent my scars even more and the shame continued to grow.

Shame locks you up on the inside and that's exactly what the enemy wants. The only thing that can combat those lies is God's Truth. So, in my anger, I went to God to wrestle this one out. A friend had spoken a word over me years before about my scars bringing a message of hope, just as it did for Thomas when Jesus showed him His own scars. A word that I didn't like but, to my annoyance, God kept on bringing to mind. So, I took that word to God and began to ask for His Truth.

As I opened my Bible I saw truth after truth. He reminded me of the scriptures He'd spoken over my life and He graciously began to restore and change how I saw myself, how I related to my body and my scars. See, His Word has the power to change us from the inside out, and that's exactly what He was doing.

I began to learn that I could own my scars, by owning my story. So, I began to own my story, and through owning my story, I began to own my scars and begin to see them for what they really were.

They are a story of God's grace, His healing power, and also a testimony of how God can take a broken life and bring restoration to those who take His hand and partner with Him. When God looks at me, He doesn't see my physical or emotional wounds, He sees me perfectly because I am a reflection of Jesus. My Heavenly Father looks at my scars and only sees Jesus.

And then one day, I heard these words, "Oh WOW! I love your arms, they are SO beautiful!" These were the words spoken from a beautiful young boy with additional needs on seeing my arms. In that moment I nearly cried because from this young boy's mouth came words that were mirroring the heart of a loving Father. That is exactly what He would say - to Him I am perfect; flaws, scars, mistakes and all.

In the end, all that mattered was what my faithful Father thought of me. As I continued to look into my Bible and see how He saw me, my own reflection changed. The deeper and more anchored I became in Him, the less I cared about the thoughts and perceptions of others. The less I cared about the perception of others, the more I found I could reflect Jesus to those around me. Whether through my work in helping bring debt relief to vulnerable individuals, or even as I cross paths with strangers in my day-to-day life, I have found that the more I see myself the way He sees me, the less people only see my scars - they now see hope, too.

Don't get me wrong, the challenges come when I am still unfairly judged by my scars, but every time this happens, I forgive and go back to the truths and promises that God continues to speak over me.

I've allowed my scars to become His testimony. So when those questions come, I have my answer ready. My scars have become a testimony of hope to others that are struggling. My scars are an open door to tell others about Jesus. The scars on my arms reflect Him, just as the scars on His hands, reflect me."

Joanna's Story

"I was asked by a young woman I work with a question I have been asked more times than I care to count, "What's wrong with your eye?"

She wasn't being rude and I didn't take it as though she was - through her autism she was trying to process the world as she saw it and didn't have the same inhibition as other people. I smiled and gave my usual "I was born that way," reply. She immediately said back to me, "Sorry for asking, it's just because everybody is different." Her response led me to reflect on just how different I had felt in life.

I was born with a little known and rare genetic disorder called Robinow Syndrome. It's a syndrome that affects me in often untold ways. It's a syndrome that has robbed me of my sense of hearing and makes me wear hearing aids; a syndrome that means I have no sense of smell and so can not enjoy the world to its fullest. It's a syndrome that has caused damage to my skeletal structures since birth which makes my back very painful; my bladder is so damaged I wear incontinence pads (yes I did just put that out there publicly!) and it's a syndrome that meant my uterus was never fully formed making me infertile. And yes, it is a syndrome that caused me to be born with Ptosis (the drooping of one my eyelids). Behind the response of "I was born that way," lies a jumble of untold pain.

For a long time I hated my face because I hated the one visible sign of my Robinow Syndrome, the syndrome that made me think I was created wrong. It silently stole so much from my body and made me ashamed to talk about it. For a long time I let my identity be consumed by sickness and death, and I felt shame as I looked in the mirror. I hated how different I looked and wondered what people thought of me when they saw my eyes.

I hated my face and hated my eyes, I thought they represented ugliness. Then one day a few years ago, while I was at Mercy, somebody told me my eyes are really beautiful and it threw me - my eyes would not have been something I'd have called beautiful. According to society, symmetry is beautiful and symmetrical is not something that my eyes could be described as.

But, I dared to look in the mirror, to look myself in the eyes and say that I am beautiful. I noticed whilst checking out my eyes in the mirror in front of me that when I smile, my eyes express wonderful joy, especially my drooping left eye!

I decided then, that the next time somebody asked "what's wrong with your eye?" I will refuse to respond with my usually awkward, "I was born like that" and respond with, "Nothing is wrong with my eyes, I love my eyes! But, let me tell you how I've come to believe that."

I now work in Alternative Provision Schools where I work with young people who can't access standard education because of behavioural and mental health needs. I am also doing a Masters Degree in Trauma Theology at Theological College and I hope to train as a Religious Studies and Citizenship teacher. I come into contact with so many people every day who feel that their differences have disqualified them in some way from being happy or finding belonging, or purpose. Maybe my smile and the joy expressed in my eyes will help them see that it is those very differences that allow us to stand out and as we stand out, we can begin to show the way for others."

A hope and a future

I included these stories to give you hope, to encourage and inspire you to become all that God has called you to be. I pray that you will know that no matter what your past looks like; good, bad or ugly - your future is one of hope, of purpose and of destiny.

This hope and this future is not just for our own benefit - let's not become so engrossed in our own journey, by our own need to find a true reflection, that we lose sight of those whose reflections are not only distorted but completely shattered.

Let's keep pressing into God, let's keep finding our identity, security and value in who He says we are, because when that happens in our lives - when we start living in the truth of His true mirror image of us - we become those who can reflect the glory of His face and so help others break free from false reflections.

Go through, then help through

——

I like adventure. I like challenges. I like to try new things and have exciting experiences. Which makes me someone that says ' yes' a lot.

"Want to jump out of a plane to celebrate your 40th?"
"Yes!"

"Want to ski down the mountain headfirst and see how fast we can go?"
"Yes!" *(60 mph by the way).*

"Want to go galloping along the beach on horseback
(in France where they have no health and safety rules)?"
"Yes!"

"Want to do a 12 mile obstacle course called Tough Mudder with 28 obstacles designed to kill you?"
"Yes! Wait...what?!"

Too late.
I was signed up and booked in and there was no going back.

Devised by the British Special Forces, Tough Mudder is 12 miles of hell (that's what they call it really!) There are walls to get over that are so high you can only climb them by standing on people's shoulders. There are ice-cube filled containers to wade through. There are cold, dirty rivers to cross and live electric wires to electrocute you. And they call it 'Mudder' because there are points during the course where the mud is so thick, it falls off of you in giant blobs of smelliness, tripping you up as you try to keep running the distance. This was quite possibly the stupidest idea I had ever said yes to.

And yet I did it anyway. And I'm glad I did. We need things in our lives that ask more from us than we are sometimes willing to give. We need opportunities to push up against our self-imposed restrictors and take a step or two outside of our comfort zone (or should it be called control zone?) We need to be those who cultivate the discipline it takes to train mentally, physically and spiritually to accomplish great feats we would ordinarily never even try.

And as it happens, I learnt a few things along the way. For instance, I learnt the importance of self-discipline and preparation. For six months before the event, I trained on the Yorkshire moors, in the cold, in the rain, in the biting wind, I went running (I HATE running) and never once did I want to do it. But I did it anyway, because it was good for me, because if I didn't train, I would again be the victim of my own stupidity.

Too many people in life fall victim to their own lack of self-discipline and lack of preparation. They want the end result but are not prepared to do what it takes to get there. They want the victory but not the battle, the fitness but not the training, the qualification but not the study. They want a true mirror image, but don't look in God's mirror to find it. The truth is, you rarely get one without the other, and so I chose to train.

At the start of the obstacle course, they give you a pep talk. And it's not what you'd expect. They tell you Tough Mudder is not a competition - it's an endurance test. And the people next to you, whether you know them or not, are not your competitors, they are your teammates.

They will be the ones alongside you when you are at your most tired, your hungriest and your coldest. The course has been specifically designed for you not to be able to complete it alone, and so they tell you the golden rule - you go through, then you help through.

Simple. You gratefully receive a helping hand from the person in front of you as you complete your obstacle, and then you turn around and help the person who is right behind you. Whether you know them or not, and whether you like them or not. Those are the rules and in looking back, I like the rules.

I think life's rules should include that simple yet profound step: we go through, and then we help through. This book is that; it's my way of having gone through a few things, faced a few obstacles and now, having got over them, wanting to reach out my hand and help you over yours.

My ask is that you do the same.

So, train hard and work hard to get over the obstacles in your way, like in the stories you've been reading about - and when you do, help someone over theirs. Smile at someone, tell your story, lend a hand, say a prayer, let someone stand on your shoulders or reach out your hand and let's make a way to climb over these obstacles - together.

About Mercy UK

Mercy UK is committed to seeing hope restored and lives transformed in partnership with the local church across the UK. Our services include:

- Effective discipleship resources,
- Pastoral support service and training
- Residential homes (for young women with life-controlling issues).

MPower Training

MPower is our one-day training course resourcing Christian people-helpers with tools and principles to support others effectively. These days are held at Mercy UK and around the UK in partnership with local churches. If you are interested in hosting a day or finding out more information about a training day near you - get in touch.

Email: partnership@mercyuk.org

Support Services

Our Support Services team provide remote support via email or phone for any individual struggling with a life controlling issue or for parents/pastors/people helpers supporting those individuals.

Please get in touch if you are seeking support or advice for yourself or for an individual you are supporting.

Email: supportservices@mercyuk.org

Resources

Further books and teaching material can be accessed via our *website: mercyuk.org*

Residential Discipleship Home

Dealing with the root causes of your behaviour is not easy but it is worth it. Our free of charge, six-month residential discipleship home exists to provide opportunities for women to experience God's unconditional love, forgiveness and life-transforming power. If you are female, aged between 18 and 30 (ish) and seeking freedom from life-controlling issues - please get in touch.

Email: intake@mercyuk.org

Speaking engagements

Mercy UK are passionate about equipping the local church. Our team speak on national and international platforms imparting to the church with messages of hope and transformation. If you would like one of our team to come and speak at your church, conference or meeting, we would love to partner with you.

Email: partnership@mercyuk.org

Give or Donate

Mercy UK is funded completely by the generosity of faithful partners, churches and other ministries. Together, we raise over £1 million and our work is impossible without these individuals and organisations. To make a donation or find out more about how you can partner with Mercy UK call

+44 (0) 1535 642 042.
Email: info@mercyuk.org

Further information on any of these areas can be found at mercyuk.org or by contacting the office on *01535 642 042* or through email at *info@mercyuk.org.*